humanism *versus* THEISM

J. A. C. FAGGINGER AUER

JULIAN HARTT

THE IOWA STATE UNIVERSITY PRESS

1 9 8 1

Printed by The Iowa State University Press, Ames, Iowa 50010

This paperback edition is an unabridged republication of the work originally published by The Antioch Press in 1951, to which has been added an introduction by E. D. Klemke.

Library of Congress Cataloging in Publication Data

Auer, J. A. C. Fagginger (Johannes Abraham Christoffel Fagginger), 1882–
   Humanism versus theism.

    1. Humanism. 2. Theism. I. Hartt, Julian Norris. II. Title.
B821.A83   1981   211'.6   81–13675
ISBN 0–8138–0916–9   (pbk.)   AACR2

CONTENTS

v

AN INTRODUCTION

The controversy between humanism and theism has been going on in one form or another for at least 2,500 years—and perhaps longer. The debate has intensified in the twentieth century, and one of the most interesting and lively instances of it is found in this book.

What is humanism, and what is theism? Characterizations of each vary to some extent. So let us concentrate on those that pertain to the present debate.

Theism, of course, is the view that a God exists. More specifically, traditional theism is the view that God is a being "than which nothing greater can be conceived." That is, God is absolute and perfect. He is all-powerful, all-knowing, infinite, eternal, supremely good, and possesses every perfection. In many theistic conceptions, God is also deemed to be personal, loving, and the creator of the universe. In this perspective, man—and indeed the whole universe—is finite and dependent upon God. In many theistic conceptions, it is thought that the duty of men and women is to serve and obey God.

According to the above characterization of theism, it follows (as Julian Hartt points out) that, although a religion may be theistic, theism is not identical with religion, or with a religion. For theism is a metaphysical belief concerning that which is ultimately real—and it is a belief about the role and significance of human life in relation to the rest of the universe. It follows from this that a person could be a theist and yet not a participant in any formal religion such as Christianity, or Judaism.

However, in spite of this distinction, the debate between humanism and theism in western culture has focused on theism as it occurs within the context of a particular religion, most notably Christianity. And indeed this is the context for the debate presented in this volume. In his defense of theism, Hartt identifies it as an essential component of Christianity.

Many criticisms of theism have been offered, from varying perspectives and approaches. A large number of these fall under the heading of humanism. What is humanism? As the term suggests, it is a philosophy that places humans at the center of the universe. It is the view that the chief end of human life is the happiness and enhancement of man upon the planet Earth and within the larger realm of Nature. Humanism either denies the central claim of theism, that God exists, or maintains that the concept of God is superfluous.

I have thus far characterized humanism in broad strokes. Most humanists subscribe to all or most of the following specific tenets. (1) The natural world is the totality of that which exists. (2) Humans are evolutionary by-products of the workings of Nature. (3) Human consciousness is dependent upon bodily functioning; hence men and women are not immortal. (4) A human being can mature and solve problems through reason and the scientific method. (5) All values are grounded within the natural universe. (6) The highest goal for moral striving is the happiness and enhancement of human life here on Earth. (7) The best social orders are those which allow for and contribute to the freedom and welfare of human beings as individuals.

In 1948 Antioch College sponsored a debate on humanism versus theism. Professor J. A. C. Fagginger Auer of Harvard Divinity School and Professor Robert Calhoun of Yale Divinity School were invited to speak on the question: "Is Humanism the Religion of the Future?" The sponsors desired to have the addresses made more widely available by the printed word. Professor Auer expanded his original lecture, and Professor Calhoun nominated Professor Julian Hartt of Yale Divinity School to present the theistic position. The Antioch Press published Professor Auer's and Professor Hartt's essays in *Humanism Versus Theism* in 1951. Although most humanists—as well as theists—would no longer think of humanism as a religion in any sense, nevertheless I still find this book to be one of the best ever written on the subject of humanism and theism.

E. D. KLEMKE
Professor of Philosophy
Iowa State University

March, 1981

FOREWORD

One of the products of the freedom of inquiry in religion which prevails at Antioch College is a constant trial-by-combat of the relative worth of humanism and theism for the needs of mankind in our age. Believing that searching bears its best fruits when contending philosophies are expounded by their ablest advocates, the Religion Committee of the College in 1948 invited Professor J. A. C. F. Auer of Harvard Divinity School and Professor Robert L. Calhoun of Yale Divinity School to confront one another here on the question: "Is Humanism the Religion of the Future?" Their addresses and the ensuing give-and-take proved so helpful to our understanding that we thought it appropriate to offer others, by printed word, something of the same opportunity. Professor Calhoun nominated Professor Julian Hartt of Yale Divinity School to represent theism in this enterprise, and Professor Auer agreed to expand his original lecture for this use.

Humanism and theism are by no means the only ideas one needs to examine to arrive at a wise and well-oriented philosophy of religion. There are those theisms, of both East and West, which conceive the divine as nonpersonal. There are Neo-Thomism and Protestant fundamentalism and agnosticism and other systems subtle and nameless, as well as positions whose differences from one another turn on issues other than the nature or existence of the divine. This little volume, then, is a modest resource for those who are searching for a religious orientation. It aims to aid and stimulate their quest, not to end it.

MORRIS T. KEETON

Yellow Springs, Ohio
April 20, 1950

humanism *versus* THEISM

PART ONE

I. The Case of Humanism

A DISCUSSION concerning humanism and its influence upon religious thinking cannot be successfully undertaken until we have a proper understanding of the meaning of the term. This creates a difficulty, because this system of thought is rather impatient of definition and, indeed, prides itself upon the fact that it is so much alive that it cannot be forced into a straitjacket of limiting terms. Hence the number of definitions is great and a choice among them is not easy.[1] For the purposes of the present discussion we shall understand humanism to be "a system of thought which assigns predominant interest to the affairs of man as compared with the superhuman, and which believes man to be capable of controlling those affairs."

The word "predominant" in our definition is used advisedly. Its purpose is to guard against the impression that humanism limits its attention wholly to occurrences within the life of a single individual, or a number of individuals, apart from a consideration of the milieu in which each human life is placed. A picture without frame lacks depth and therefore meaning. The significance of a human life cannot be explained apart from the universe which surrounds it, since it is obviously impossible to determine the nature of anything apart from its relations.

But humanism insists that the frame gains its importance from the picture which it encircles and not the picture from the frame; from a human point of view it is the universe which gets

---

[1] J. A. C. Fagginger Auer, *Humanism States Its Case,* (American Unitarian Association, 1933).

3

its importance from touching our life, not our life which gains
its significance chiefly by reason of its relation to the universe.

With regard to this matter humanism differs fundamentally
from theism. The latter teaches that the greater lends significance
to the lesser, that power gives meaning to weakness, infinitude
to finitude, God to man. Humanism contends that each thing,
great or small, has intrinsic value which, since it pertains to the
thing itself, cannot be borrowed. A grain of sand, within the limitations set to it, is as important as the planet of which it is a part.
Humanism therefore insists that to each man his own life is important for what it is in and by itself, and that all else borrows its
meaning from it, brief though our existence on earth may be.
Therefore all considerations must start from it: we should reason
from the center to the circumference and not from the circumference to the center—from a human life to the universe, not
from the universe to a human life.

The proper method of approach is in fact the most important
factor in our entire investigation of reality. By a proper method
humanists understand a method suitable for men, that is, for
beings constituted as we are, not for the absolute or for creatures
possessing a mind essentially different from our own. This follows from the conviction, in which all humanists share, that the
concept of truth has no meaning apart from a human consciousness for which it is true. Truth is conformity with reality, without doubt; but reality presupposes the existence of a mind for
which it is real, in this case the human mind; in no other sense
can the term be said to have any meaning for us. The Absolute
may have his manner of approach to the real; but it is not ours,
nor can it be. Hence we need take no account of it.

Do we know of a method which has yielded successful results
in our search for the truth? We do; it is the method of trial-and-
error. Its success has been due negatively to the mistakes it has
avoided and positively to its mode of applying logical principles
to the discovery of that which as yet was unknown.

The main fallacy avoided by the trial-and-error method is that of begging the question. No one can hope to arrive at a sound conclusion in reasoning when his mind is already made up before he starts his investigation. Theism is guilty of this fallacy because it starts with a belief in the existence of God before it has given adequate proof that this existence is a reality; in other words, it assumes as a fact a matter which is still in doubt. An unproved assumption cannot serve as the basis for a sound argument. Humanism does not criticize theism because it believes in the existence of a personal God but because it announces this belief as based upon an undoubted fact before it has a right to do so. A belief in a personal God is a conclusion. Conclusions belong at the end of an argument and not at its beginning.

It is evident that no investigation concerning the nature of reality can be started without allowing for some assumptions; we need to take for granted, for instance, the fact of our own existence, and it must also be assumed that the process of human reasoning is adequate to human needs. If we should doubt the reality of our existence or believe that human reasoning is bound to lead to error, as did John Calvin with regard to matters pertaining to religion, there would be little use in starting any inquiry.

We should, however, adapt Occam's well-known "law of parsimony" to our particular case and start from the smallest possible number of assumptions, each one of which must be inevitable if reasoning is to take place at all.[2] If we assume more than is necessary, the excessive number of assumptions will become an obstruction in the way of progress rather than an aid. An engine is the more efficient in proportion to its simplicity.

It is quite clear that theism does not follow this practice. Its chief postulate, the existence of God, is no necessary basis for argument, in the same sense in which a belief in the trustworthiness

---

[2] Compare: Edwin Arthur Burtt, *Principles and Problems of Right Thinking,* (Harper, 1931), Chapters IV and V.

of human reason is that. Such a postulate is therefore more than is required in order to reach valid conclusions regarding the truth, and being a "too-much" it is no help but a hindrance in this matter. It could, of course, become an asset, but not until the content of the belief has become a proved fact; then it might become a valuable link in our chain of reasoning. But when in this chain matters of fact and mere assumptions are linked together as though they had the same value, confusion results and eventually the chain will break at its weakest point, which is always the place where we find an unproved assumption.

Having started our investigation by assuming as little as possible, we continue it after the same manner. From the beginning till the end of the argument the *lex parsimoniae* should rule; all that is not needed for the purpose of clarification and explanation should be eliminated, and all alleged facts which have not proved themselves to be real facts should be excluded for the time being. Thereafter, reasoning by analogy—i.e., by comparing the known with the unknown for the sake of discovering similarities—we should slowly move forward until a valid conclusion is reached. It is important to remember that in all instances the unknown is to be explained by the aid of the known and never the known by the aid of the unknown. Since man is known and God is unknown, the concept of man should serve in explanation of the concept of God and not the other way around.[3] At this point theism and humanism take sharp issue.

Theism condemns this method. It admits that its use has led to the gaining of valuable results in all fields where only purely human factors are concerned; but religion is more than that, it includes the superhuman. By the very fact that ultimate truths are involved, religion stands alone in all fields of human interest. Therefore in the religious field human reason is inadequate; the weighing and measuring process of science breaks down; the

---

[3] That this has actually happened is amply proved by the history of the development of the God concept from earliest times to the present moment.

normal processes of human logic fail. We are dealing with the supernatural and we can approach it only by the avenue of faith. Moreover theism reminds us that the scientific method, even within the limits of the field in which it may be legitimately used, claims far more for itself than is justified by the results. Observation, hypothesis, implication and verification, the four steps involved in the procedure, do not lead to absolute certainty. Such certainty, Hume reminded us, would involve complete knowledge of causal relations between things, events and circumstances which our experience does not supply. All we are able to discover is a succession of phenomena in a given order, which does not seem to vary in the course of time. This leads us to believe that the succession of events rests on necessity, but we are by no means justified in reaching such a conclusion. B may have followed A for centuries, but there is no way of disproving that some time in the future it may disassociate itself from A altogether and follow J. Professor Trueblood quite convincingly supports the contention that the use of the scientific method can provide us with a high degree of probability but can go no further.[4]

Humanism fully agrees with this statement, but it would urge that the shortcomings of the scientific method do not prove the strength of the method which theism employs; the substitution of faith for exploration and experimentation brings no gain.

Granted that science can give us no absolute certainty, it has rendered us a significant service when it has provided us with a high degree of probability. By doing so it has given us in fact all the certainty which a human being can hope to have. This foundation supports the ever expanding structure of human knowledge which has borne concrete fruit in a thousand ways to the undeniable welfare of mankind. What better evidence of its worth can be advanced?

Can theism prove its contentions with the same degree of cer-

---

[4] D. E. Trueblood, *The Logic of Belief,* (Harper, 1942), Chapter III, "The Nature of Evidence."

tainty? Can it furnish us with a high degree of probability? Do
theist arguments have the same measure of general validity? Are
its teachings so compelling that, should anyone deny them, he
would justly fall under the condemnation of illogical reasoning,
or worse, of flying in the face of facts?

Humanism maintains that the answer to all of these questions is "no," and many theists would agree with this verdict. But
in fairness one ought to inquire whether these questions posed
by humanists are justified. We are, after all, dealing with an entirely different set of data from those with which science is oper-
ating; and we cannot therefore demand that theistic theology
shall use the same *modus operandi* in dealing with its facts which
science uses within the field of its interest. Any set of facts in a
given relation imposes upon the one trying to understand it a
method of approach which is consistent with its character. Colors
demand to be seen, sounds to be heard, and food to be tasted.
A blind man cannot understand a picture nor a deaf man a
melody.

Religious facts do not reach us as a result of a discovery made
by the human mind in the same sense in which Newton discovered the law of gravity. Therefore one cannot establish their veracity by subjecting them to a kind of laboratory test in which
check and countercheck play a part. They are intuitive certainties, akin to the clear and precise ideas which play such an important role in the Cartesian system. It is not their reasonableness
which first of all convinces us of their worth; we are forced to
accept them in the end because they are persistent, because they
will not be denied. They do not argue with us; they place us before a practical alternative: "accept us," they say, "and you will
find rest for your soul; deny us and your soul will know no rest."

Since the avenue of understanding is barred, we must find
another pathway toward religious certainty; the only one open is
the road of faith. If we cannot know the "why" of things, which
is the function of understanding, we can at least know the "that,"

which is the function of faith; or putting it differently, we can learn to know that religious truths are real although we shall never comprehend the reason for their existence.

There is in the theistic approach a fair share of pragmatism: a given belief works in a human life; therefore it must have a foundation in concrete reality. The popular argument for the existence of God, which occasionally one still encounters, and which derives its force from the universal assent of the human race, is a case in point. All men agree that God exists, because intuitively they feel that it must be so; hence what their intuitions tell them as being so corresponds to a concrete fact.

The argument is not without merit. Our intuitions are not likely to fool us. If they did, life would not be possible at all, since nine-tenths of it depends upon what the intuitions tell us. It is also true that these intuitive reactions to mental stimuli are fairly uniform among men. Therefore, our first impulse with regard to an intuitive notion is that it is the truth, and very often it is.

But one cannot transfer experiences on one level of conscious life to another without making some allowance for differences. The matters about which theism is arguing are not intuitional, surely not in the form in which they are presented. The doctrine is not limited to the general notion that the universe is bound to give some support to the creatures which it brought forth; even humanism within certain limits would not deny this notion. The theistic system goes beyond this, however. It is highly complex, and it has a great deal to say about the *nature* of the supporting power. It tells us that God, the supporting power, is a person, and that, even though this may seem inconsistent with the notion of personality, God is a person who knows no limits either as to space, time, power, or knowledge. It goes on to say that the support which God gives each of us is not of a general nature, in the sense in which the law of gravity affects all things alike, but that it is specific, purposeful, and therefore essentially different in the case of each individual. God is a father; He is interested in each one of us in the manner in which a human father is interested in his children. He wishes to guard us from evil and lead us in the direction of the good, and His final purpose is the victory of good over evil so that there shall be no further vexing problems for us to solve.

That assuredly is what theism teaches. That is the doctrine which the man in the pews expects his minister to preach, or which at least he takes for granted his minister would preach should he deal with this specific problem. Should he ever hear his pastor say that the relation between God and men is precisely the same as the one between a natural law and the objects which it affects, he would be either puzzled or indignant, probably both. He would tell the minister that he did not go to church to hear that kind of thing, and that in his judgment the pastor would do well to leave the ministry. Many individual deviations on the part of certain clergymen from this point of view may be accepted by the people in the pews, but it is obviously impossible to deal with each of these separately. For the purposes of discussion we must interpret the term theism in the traditional sense, in the sense in which it is accepted by laiety, and in the manner in which it is still explained in the doctrinal utterances of the various churches.

As such, the basic assumptions of theism are more in number than those of humanism, and they are also far more detailed. It follows that they require a greater measure of evidence in order to give them substance. But it is this very evidence which is admittedly lacking. No proof for the existence of God has yet been advanced which is universally persuasive, much less for the existence of a personal God interested in each one of His creatures and concerned about their individual welfare.

Hence certainty regarding these matters must be gained in a way different from the one which we normally follow. We must allow our intuitions to function. Faith and hope will do for us what patient scientific research cannot do. They will give us certainty, although the process by which we arrived at this state of mind will never be revealed to us. But what matter, as long as the desired result is obtained?

Moreover, thus theism tells us, this certainty is so complete that the fear of its being upset is wholly dissipated. The man who accepts the truth in faith has no fear that his intellect will ever disprove what he has accepted as true. The intellect is slower than the intuitions; in the fullness of time it will support their findings, but it will never prove them mistaken. To that extent the way of faith is better than the way of knowledge. He who believes has his intellectual doubts stilled, even if he does not quite know how; but he who knows can never be quite sure that his knowledge will not be upset. And it is important to know that this acme of surety may be had in the very field where human knowledge is powerless, in the realm of religion.

Humanism does not deny that through the exercise of faith a sense of certainty may be gained, but it would submit that this experience is subjective. It happens that the matter in dispute between theism and humanism touches the question of existence: either God is or He is not; after-life is a fact or it is no fact. In any argument where a possible existence is opposed to a possible non-existence subjective opinions should play no part. There is either a desk in my study or there is none; no subjective opinion changes that fact.

Theism, however, does not state that its doctrine is subjective in its character; on the contrary it deems its teachings to be in accordance with the actual facts so that they have the character of universally valid propositions. Hence theism does not say, "*some people* believe that God is," but "*God is*," or "*some people* have reached the conclusion that immortality is a fact," but "everlasting life is a reality." A missionary going to a foreign field would scarcely tell the heathen that his message might be true or not, depending upon some bits of information which, it was hoped, might be forthcoming.

To the extent to which the statements made by theism are coldly factual in their nature, they differ not a whit from the proposition "the sum of the three angles of a triangle is equal to two right angles," and they demand the same kind of proof; they must, I repeat, either be supported by the evidence of the senses or else by irrefutable logic.

This support they do not get and, theism admits, they cannot get. Therefore the structure of argument must be shored up some other way. This theism attempts to do, but the props prove weak because the reasons adduced in support of the position defeat themselves. On examination we discover them to be variations of the logical fallacy of begging the question, or else they derive from wish thinking.

The most common argument is still that God must exist because He has revealed that fact directly to given individuals or else, by indirection, through Holy Scripture. This claim plainly begs the question because it assumes the existence of a God who can reveal Himself beyond doubt or argument, which is the very matter which is in dispute. So-called personal revelations, moreover, provide flimsy evidence; they are often called upon to support wholly contradictory claims. The testimony of Scripture will have no weight with those who do not believe the Bible to be the inspired Word of God.

Reference is often made to a revelation regarding the existence of God which comes to us from nature. It is a slightly different argument from the ones with which I have been concerned. Its appeal is not to the emotions or to intuition, but rather to the intellect. It differs only in degree from the well-known cosmological and the theological proofs, which since the days of Kant have been liabilities rather than assets even to theistic theology. At present it suffices to say that no argument in support of the Divine existence drawn from nature is universally compelling.

But the most common line of reasoning used by theism in proof of the veracity of its teachings is an indirect one. We are invited to consider the consequences which would follow from the nonexistence of God. We are told that without God life would not be worth living because it would have no meaning. We are assured that in a godless world there would be no valid norms for action since man-created standards would vary from year to year. Thus our social life would be without foundation; it would become disorganized beyond the possibility of redemption.

Moreover, theism wishes us to remember that the greatest minds of the ages have accepted the Divine existence as a fact. Is it likely that Jesus, Paul, St. Augustine and Luther would have been in error regarding the central dogma in their entire system of thought? It seems scarcely possible.

The answer to these arguments suggests itself readily. A thing does not exist because it is desirable that it should exist. The fact that I need a million dollars to carry on my business is no proof that I either have this amount or will ever get it. If it be true that life has no meaning without God, as the theists aver, the correct inference is that human existence may be meaningless, not that God must exist in order to give life meaning.

Incidentally the assertion that human existence derives its meaning only from God is itself a statement in need of proof. Many who cannot accept the theistic doctrine find life highly worth while; they discover many valid norms for action; and they do not despair about the ultimate disruption of our social life, to which their constant interest in social activity bears witness. In the final summing up of the case their judgment should receive its appropriate measure of attention; surely the matter is not quite so easily settled as some theists would have you suppose.

And finally the appeal to authority, to the opinions of men who rank far above the average, is more likely to lead to confusion of the issue than to its clarification. Great men have been wrong about many things. We do not accept St. Augustine's cosmography; why should we necessarily accept his theology? He was a great theologian, in the sense that he dealt most efficiently with the material at his disposal; but he was subject to the limitations of his time. The fifth century cannot be allowed to legislate for the twentieth century, even in matters of theology.

The arguments which theism uses do not support its contentions, at least not in the manner in which they are stated. These teachings are presented to us in a factual manner. They are specific, clear, and concrete; indeed theism boasts about the fact that its creed presents nothing either provisional or hypothetical. It therefore requires the kind of support which all specific, clear, and concrete statements demand before they can be admitted to square with the facts. This solid foundation theism cannot provide.

Humanism does not condemn theism because it indulges in wish thinking or because it relies heavily upon its intuitions. There is nothing wrong with either of these things. If our wishes had not incited us to constant activity, if persistently we had disregarded the counsel of our intuitions, we should still be living in caves. Wish thinking does not necessarily lead to error, but it furnishes no trustworthy method for arriving at the truth; it is like an automibile without a proper steering apparatus; you may get to your destination, but you are taking chances.

The trouble with theism is that it does not use the method which fits its needs. Therefore it is taking chances and sometimes unwarranted chances. Humanism is more prudent in this respect. Like theism it is trying to discover clear and concrete facts; and in order to obtain those it uses the only method through which such facts can be gained, the method which science uses. Obviously its claims are more modest than those of theism and perhaps somewhat more provisional, but they are not so easily upset.

II. Humanism and the Problem of Religion

THE SIXTEENTH CHAPTER of the Book of Acts tells us the story of the incarceration of Paul and Silas. As the result of a miraculous earthquake the prisoners are released and the jailer, afraid that some may have made their escape, is about to take his life. Then Paul tells him that he must do himself no injury since all of the prisoners are there. Though reassured on this point the keeper is still greatly upset; at least we are told that he falls down before Paul and Silas exclaiming, "Sirs, what shall I do to be saved?"

What does he mean? It is not easy to translate the Greek word σώζω in this passage. Is he concerned about the salvation of his soul? A man just released from the fear of physical death is scarcely in a mental condition to inquire the next moment about a method through which his soul might be rendered safe, such reflections belong to the more quiet moments of life. Though the jailer is reputed to have become a Christian that same day, being baptized into the faith with his entire family, the salvation which concerned him at first was more likely freedom from punishment which might well have followed the upset in prison.

But Paul does not take it thus; he believes that the jailer is seeking to find a way toward spiritual salvation. And his answer is, "Believe on the Lord Jesus Christ." Salvation, therefore is the result of believing in something, something not about yourself but about someone else. Salvation comes from the outside. This is a typical notion in the theistic system of theology of which Paul is but an early representative.

15

The traditional view of theism regarding the function of religion is, that it is intended to save you from the effect of the unfortunate circumstances in the midst of which you are placed and which you cannot change by your own power. It therefore points to a source of power outside of you, infinitely greater than your own, and capable of dealing with any problem. That such a reservoir of power exists you should believe, and this very belief will save you from further evil.

True, theism as we know it today through most of its representatives, does not teach that mere belief is enough; its counsel is *ora et labora*. But we are warned that a human being who believes that he can solve his problems unaided is guilty, not only of grievous error but also of a major sin.

If you but grant the first assumptions made by theism, its explanation of the function of religion is perfectly natural and logical. If we concede that a man cannot change basically the conditions among which he lives, then to attempt to do so is a sinful waste of time. You not only indulge in needless effort, but through your wilfulness you prevent yourself from grasping the only chance of obtaining security and peace of mind which is offered you, and which is conditioned upon your seeking the source whence true peace and security flow. If a man suffering from scarlet fever deliberately uses a medicine which is meant for frostbite, he is wasting time, money and effort; whereas by taking the proper medicine he might be cured.

Not without reason Bell writes: "Since there is no significance for man in terms of progress, since man cannot solve his own problem by pulling at his bootstraps, man must and can be saved from futility only by the intervention of God. Christianity is a religion of redemption, divine redemption of man from an otherwise inevitable inanity."[1] While Reinhold Niebuhr has this to say: "Every facet of the Christian revelation, whether of the relation of God to history, or of the relation of man to the eternal,

---

[1] Bernard Iddings Bell, *Atlantic Monthly*, January, 1946.

points to the impossibility of man fulfilling the true meaning of his life, and reveals sin to be primarily derived from his abortive efforts to do so." [2]

Pure Calvinism—witness John Calvin's *Institutes*—will furnish a hundred examples of the same mode of reasoning; but, if its first premises are granted, it is inescapable in its logic.

What is the first assumption upon which theism bases all of its teachings? It is a belief that in matters of the spirit the pattern is wholly different from the one which we discover in the material world. The relations between facts in the two fields are unlike and therefore the results derived from the two sets of factual relations dissimilar. A single example may serve to illustrate this. Our physical health is constantly endangered. We are always threatened by small organisms, microbes, which might do us harm, but which are prevented from doing so by substances which the body itself creates for this precise purpose. By developing antibodies the human body keeps the enemies out and solves its own problems. When illness does occur, because the enemy is temporarily victorious, the body does not give up the fight; but after a while, due to its recuperative powers, regains its health. That is normal. In a manner of speaking the material body lifts itself by its own bootstraps.

But, our mental life, our social life, if you will, cannot do this, at least so the theists tell us. Our spiritual body cannot develop antibodies to keep the foe out. Worse than that, it creates its own enemies; it breeds corruption, pride and error. In other words it is normal for the spiritual nature of man to be abnormal. And its greatest abnormality is, and here Calvin would nod in agreement, that on occasion it thinks itself to be normal; and that, as a result of this delusion, it tries to create within itself unaided forces which might counteract evil.

Why the source of all being should have used two such utterly

---

[2] Reinhold Niebuhr, *Nature and Destiny of Man*, (Scribner, 1941), Vol. II, p. 98.

contradictory methods to carry out His purposes remains a mystery. Of course, the answer on the part of the theists is that God never intended that our spirit should thus be corrupted. Perhaps, —but who thwarted God's original intention? Man? But that would make him as powerful as God, indeed more powerful, because man's evil will would then have shown itself to be strong enough to overcome God's good intentions. If Satan proves to be stronger than God, those who worship Satan show good sense; for strength, the power to carry out the plans intended, is the essential characteristic of Godhood. He who has no strength to rule does not deserve to be King.

The problem defies solution. We are left with a God whose actions are incomprehensible because they are contradictory, and with a man who lives on two levels of existence, the material and the spiritual one, which are mutually exclusive. The situation is hopeless.

But the situation is hopeless only because it does not represent real conditions but artificial ones. The difference between a real problem and an unreal one is that the first one contains within itself the possibility of solution whereas the second one does not. An attempt to square the circle is an endeavor to deal with an unreal problem, hence one cannot hope for success.

Theism presents many artificial problems, not unlike the one of trying to square the circle, and most of its difficulties are referable to that fact. Many of its assumptions are not real; moreover, they beg the question; therefore, they create difficulties for which there is no cure.

The assumption that man's moral nature is incapable of dealing with the matter of evil, unless supported by some higher power, is a theory which cannot be established in fact. No one denies that man sins, and that, a few perfectionists to the contrary, he probably will continue to do so from time to time. But the presence of sin does not prove that man is essentially sinful, in the sense that it is more normal for him to sin than to do good.

If that had been the case there would be no human society at all, even an imperfect one. Whenever the minus signs outnumber the plus signs, life in any form becomes an impossibility. Whatever has existed over a long time, and that is true of man, must have more positive qualities than negative ones. It pays to reexamine history with that fact in mind.

The concept of religion to which theism clings is not well founded, in the sense that it is the result of actually tested experience, and to that extent at least it is arbitrary. Therefore everything connected with it is more or less arbitrary. The notions of sin, virtue, salvation and regeneration receive an artificial and therefore an unconvincing explanation. This is only to be expected: if you start with an ill-founded idea, you cannot expect well-founded results in thought. The ill-founded assumption that two plus two are equal to six will lead to the equally erroneous supposition that two plus two plus two are equal to nine.

But, though not well-founded, the theistic system is unquestionably logical: logical in its content, once the first assumptions are admitted; logical too in its mode of procedure. If God is the only source of truth, then human thinking should be guided by the information which flows from that source, and it should not set up standards of its own. Nor is there need for such "creaturely activity." God, through His revelation, provides us with all the facts we need to know. He tells us of His purposes regarding ourselves. He gives us an inkling concerning His ultimate plan with creation. He tells us something regarding the method of salvation it pleases Him to use. He makes us acquainted with the norms for moral behavior, and therefore by inference with the nature of immoral action.

That should suffice. True, the human spirit rebels against the fact that man is wholly passive in this scheme of things, that its opinion is never invited. But, why should it be invited? Why should Infinite Wisdom ask counsel of ignorance?

It does not do to say that this picture of theistic theology is changed, that it represents the view of Calvin in the *Institutes* from which long ago we have departed. When Barth tells us that there is a way from God to man but no way from man to God, when Niebuhr counts it sin that man should arrogantly believe that he has the correct answers to some of the problems of life and death, they are not far removed from Calvin. For they too operate with the notion of the Secret Counsel of God, in which all things are ultimately decided independently of human wishes.

God legislates for man, thus theism argues—God: infinite, absolute, all knowing, all powerful, sinless, free from temptation, bound in no conceivable way by anything that can bind. He legislates for man: finite, limited, ignorant concerning the things most important to him, weak, sinful, constantly tempted, bound by all things that can bind.

There is the great theistic affirmation, impressive because it is stated forcibly and without any qualifying clauses. And yet one wonders whether the very force of the statement is not due to oversimplification through which difficulties are eliminated without justification. One is puzzled as to whether a legislator can create laws for a being which is so far removed from him as God is from man. If the conditions are as stated by the theists, one is scarcely amazed at the fact that there is no way from man to God, but one is astounded that there should be a way from God to man. Man may not be able to think God's thoughts after Him, but can God divine the thoughts of man? Understanding means that somewhere there must be a point of contact between the one desiring to understand and the object to be understood, but in this case where is it? Where could it conceivably be?

The chief object of religion is the integration of man. Theism and humanism may differ about the way in which this integration should be brought about, but both agree that man should be inwardly whole, to the extent, at least, to which this is possible. As it is, man is a "house divided against itself." The spirit wars against the flesh and the flesh against the spirit. Not without cause

Paul writes, "for what I would, that I do not, but what I hate, that do I."

The reason man is in this condition derives from the fact that he turns his back upon God, who is the principle of unity. That, theism tells us, is his error; nay more, that is his cardinal sin for which daily he receives punishment, the chastisement of feeling dissatisfied, unhappy and futile. For whoever shuts God out excludes the very power which might cause his inward discord to go, and he prevents himself from reaching the condition where will, intellect and the emotions join together toward the furthering of one supreme end.[3] Hence theism urges men constantly to come to God.

But how can men do that, and what precisely would happen if they should follow this invitation? Would God take over the work? Would He take possession of man and stop the inner warfare by some miracle? If so, one wonders why He did not do so before. Why did He not make man from the beginning in such a fashion that this inner division could not have taken place? One is rather reminded of a careless workingman who manufactures a faulty article and then is forced afterwards to do the work all over again.

But can a man be made over by a force outside of him? The answer to this question is, "yes," if we deprive man of any power of free expression so that he is reduced to the status of a thing. The answer is "no"; emphatically, "no," if he be a person. One is not surprised that in the case of extreme Calvinism man loses his personality altogether, and becomes a thing, a pawn upon the divine chessboard, which God moves forward as it pleases Him. A person can be healed only from within, never from without. True, influences from without may help toward the cure, but the final healing process is an inward one, in the same way in which medicine only helps the body to cure itself.

---

[3] J. A. C. Fagginger Auer, *Humanism States Its Case,* (American Unitarian Association, 1933), Chapter IV.

It is not easy to harmonize the idea of the essential helplessness of man with the passion for moral righteousness which is characteristic of some of the leading theists. Do their human intuitions find it hard to accept the consequences of the doctrine which some of their writings reveal? Writes Bernard Iddings Bell in his article in the *Atlantic Monthly* for January 1946, already quoted: "Natural man, apart from God, is an unreliable creature except for this; that one can always count on his getting nowhere that satisfies him in his individual living."

A strong statement, with which not all theists would agree! It overstates, some might say, the degree to which God's infinite strength is placed in opposition to man's weakness. But does it if the assumptions of theism are granted? It is really difficult to see how in the theistic system religion can be anything but a scheme on the part of God intended for the salvation of man, which calls for no cooperation on the part of man himself, except that he is asked to acknowledge the validity of the divine plan without questioning. And if this is a correct interpretation of what theists mean by religion, it is psychologically impossible that it shall ever work.

Humanism agrees that religion has for its chief object the integration of man; but it differs from theism in this, that it neither believes, nor desires, that this process shall ever be wholly completed; nor does it think that even a partial completion can be brought about by an agency outside of man.

Theism is in the habit of using absolute terms. When it talks about the integration of human personality, it thinks of it in an absolute way. It means that all problems are solved, that all inner struggle has ceased, that sin is gone, and that temptation no longer has any real meaning. If that is not what the Christian Church in its theistic form has been trying to preach, the men in the pews have been allowed to continue under a curious misconception for many centuries. For that reason Jesus, whose life was alleged to be a perfect pattern of what a human existence should be, was declared to be sinless. Surely the devil tempted Him, but it was a foregone conclusion that this attempt would fail. A perfect life is a sinless life.

Humanism thinks in relative terms. When it talks about the integration of human personality it thinks of relative stability, complete enough to do away with unnecessary friction, but not of such a character as to eliminate friction altogether. Humanism is not looking for a sinless world; the idea of the "Communion of the Saints" does not attract it, unless this concept were radically reinterpreted. A saint is but a potential sinner without imagination, and a world shorn of humor and imagination is not an inviting place in which to live.

But there is nothing lax about the moral code of the humanists; there is no room for indulgence. One would not go far wrong if one defined humanism as Puritanism with a sense of humor.

The point is that humanism refuses to think of man as essentially evil merely because he may be in error, or even deliberately at fault. Man can be thought of as essentially corrupt only when we compare him with a fictitious person, who never had, nor ever will have, existence; with a man who has solved every problem, and for whom there is nothing left to do; with the proverbial saint who has conquered all evil, so that neither sin nor temptation has any further meaning in his life. But, a man who cannot be tempted is not a moral personality. There is no morality when there is no constant need of choosing between the better and the worse. Nor does this mean that the moral man invariably, and without effort, chooses the right.

Life means overcoming resistance in every one of its aspects. Moral life signifies the constant endeavor to overcome unnecessary inward friction, which causes waste and wear, for the sake of reducing it to necessary friction; that is, to the point where the process of establishing inward harmony does not mean wear, but rather intensified life and the production of fruitful energy. Without friction no motion is possible, and therefore no life. A measure of inner division, an unstable equilibrium, a certain portion of error even, is a necessary part of man's mental makeup. It does not betoken mental corruption.

It is axiomatic that within the universe all things possess the qualities which make their individual existence possible; if they did not, they would not have entered into the state of being. There are moments when disturbances occur; a flower may look sickly for a while. That does not mean that it cannot regain its health. Man is no different, whether you consider him as a physical or a moral being. He possesses what he needs in order to exist. He has his upsets, but he is not upset all of the time, nor even most of the time. If he is to be judged, it should be done with reference to the average level of his existence and not the lowest one.

If a man were a moral misfit, it would reflect strangely upon the alleged cause of man's existence, God Himself, particularly since, being omniscient, He not only fashioned man, but also knew how His creature would turn out.

The religion which humanism teaches is not a design by which to save man from abnormality, but an attempt to preserve his essential normality. When a complicated piece of machinery is produced by a reliable factory, it is tested and retested until the producers know that it will do all that justifiably can be expected of it. When it is delivered to the purchaser, he is supposed to give it proper care. If he omits to do this, the machinery will not function; but that does not mean that the machinery was originally faulty.

Religion, functionally speaking, is a method of taking care of one of nature's products, the most complicated, the most sensitive among them all. It is the most vulnerable product too, by reason of its very complexity and sensitivity; and yet, in spite of all this, strong beyond belief, if only the inner relations are not unduly disturbed.

The object of religion is not in the first place to restore health, but to retain it. It is not there to correct error, but to prevent it. Of course, there are some who have lost their spiritual health, and who live in error already. In that case religion cannot prevent the trouble because the harm is done; then its function is to correct. But even then correction means restoration to a spiritual condition which was sound to begin with, and the conviction implied in the process of correction is that once spiritual health is regained, it may be retained. Were it otherwise, there would be little use in making the endeavor at all.

The entire religious technique of humanism is therefore essentially different from the one employed in theism. Its method is not first of all to impart information which we do not already possess, for the sake of the salvation of our souls, but to teach us to make good use of things we already know. Insofar as humanism teaches facts at all for the sake of improving, they are facts concerning man himself and not about some being outside of him. These facts, moreover, are positive; they are concerned with man's assets and not his liabilities.

When one listens to the typical prayer spoken by a minister in the pulpit, one is struck by two things which appear peculiar. First of all the minister informs the Lord regarding a number of matters with which presumably He is already acquainted; secondly God is asked to grant us a good many things which apparently He forgot to give. If, for the mere sake of the argument a humanist were to offer up prayer to the Deity, its content would be the exact reverse. He would not give God information which He did not need, and surely he would not ask God to give more than He had already given. More likely the minister would express his sorrow and shame that we, men, had left unused the abundant gifts which had already come to us.

The object of religion is to teach men to use properly what they already have. And in summing up what they do have we should be guilty neither of overstatement nor understatement; it should be our endeavor to find the average norm..

It is unfair, in fact foolish, to judge the average man by a standard so high that few can reach it, or so low that only a relatively small number descend to it. Religion is education, the education of the human race as Lessing called it. The true merit of a class of pupils is not determined by the few top men, nor by the equally few dullards at the bottom of the class, but by the average student. The whole educational scheme, the subjects chosen, the hours of study required, are determined, and rightly too, with reference to the average scholar.

When we are dealing with religion let us ask, how does the average man react to the circumstances of life; how does he meet sorrow, how good fortune, how does he face death? At what point does his moral code break down; when, and under what circumstances, does he forsake honesty for dishonesty, tolerance for intolerance, unselfishness for selfishness; and when does his affection for others change to hatred? As with a bar of steel, in the physical realm, thus with man in the moral realm, let us determine the exact breaking point.

Then, let us ask ourselves the question whether what we see man do is the highest performance of which he is capable; need the breaking point be where it is; can he do more than he is doing with what he has? Will education help him, and if so, what kind of education? Does man need to know more facts, or should he learn how to handle facts? What is the effect of a good example set by other men? Is there any way to make man more reasonable, to strengthen his will, to develop his patience, so that he will take time to see the point of view of others? Can we teach a man to do what he can and to bear what he must? Is it possible to strengthen his courage to the point where he faces even death not as a coward but with his head up?

Is it true that only those who believe in a personal God exhibit those positive and desirable qualities, whereas others lack them? If so, that would be an argument for theism. But we know, even theists would admit, that this is not the case.

Inward wholeness, it would seem, does not necessarily derive from a belief in the everlasting support from a being, other and greater than we. How does it originate? Are not the theists mistaken in the cause which they accept as the only true one? Must we not reinvestigate the whole matter of religion from the very ground up, in order to arrive at a better understanding of the factors which are operative in it? If we resolve to do this, quite objectively, should we not be better able to determine its function?

To each one of these questions humanism replies with an emphatic "yes." As long as we are trying to define the concept of man without adequately examining the factors which must be known in order to make the definition possible, we shall get nowhere. As long as our explanation of man's real nature bears reference only to saints who need solve problems no longer, or to irredeemable sinners who are constitutionally unable to solve any problems—as long as we refuse to pay attention to the norm which is found between these two, we shall get nowhere. As long as we judge man by his present performance, refusing to take into account a possible improvement resulting from a better use of his assets, we shall get nowhere.

The Dutch have a proverb worthwhile pondering: "Let each man learn to row with the oars he has got." Humanism approves. No one should borrow money for the sake of doing business unless he has to do so. Let us not borrow treasures from the realms of infinity until we actually discover that within our limited sphere we cannot find enough spiritual capital for our reasonable needs.

III. God and Man

RELIGION IS FUNCTIONAL; lacking a function it would be meaningless. The nature of its function depends upon the use which a man wishes to make of religion, and on this point men differ. It follows that religion has various focal points, which depend upon the individual interests of the men concerned. God, man, nature, society and the nation in turn have become objects of religious attention. It is a commonplace that communism is more of a religion than an economic system, and that Nazism was the same. When we find in life an object of interest so intense that, compared with it, all other matters become secondary, we have found our religion.[1]

It is obvious that we do not start in life with our religion completed: we must first find our object of interest. True, very early in life children may give indications of the type of interest they are likely to develop, but one cannot be sure. Darwin, early in life was greatly concerned with formal religion; but he lost all taste for it, and later he gave his whole mind and soul to science.

The object of our supreme attention will determine the nature of our religion. If we desire nothing better than to build up the strength of our nation, we shall revere power and all things which produce it; if we wish a well regulated society, we shall exalt justice. If our religion is directed toward God, it will show certain characteristics; if it is pointed toward man, its distinctive qualities will be different.

---

[1] J. A. C. Fagginger Auer, *Humanism States Its Case*, (American Unitarian Association), Chapter IV.

28

Why do men become interested in the idea of God? Obviously because they want God to do something for them which they cannot do for themselves. To say that men love the Deity for His own sake, apart from any influence which He may have upon their lives, is to talk psychological nonsense. Love betokens a direct and personal interest between two beings so closely connected the one with the other that if either of them should go, the life of the second would show a great loss.

What do men desire that God shall do for them? The answer has already been given: they desire Him to solve problems for them which they themselves are incapable of settling. If there were no problems that demanded a solution, it is not likely that the idea of God would have emerged; man would have trusted his own powers.

But there are such problems; there are puzzling questions to be answered, and in consequence the idea of a God did emerge. It is interesting that the nature of the problems given to God for solution has changed in the course of time. When man was utterly unable to control the forces of nature, God was asked to do that for him. But this is no longer the case; we try to do that ourselves in our laboratories. When the science of medicine did not exist, the priests were called upon to perform their strange rites to force mysterious powers of the air to come to our aid; but here too the matter has changed. It is noteworthy that due to the fact that man is better able to help himself, the number of things for which we implore divine assistance has been reduced to only a fraction of what it used to be.

But there are certain matters left with which we cannot deal, and which are of such a nature that it is not likely that we shall ever be able to control them. Death is the greatest of them all, and, within life, sorrow, illness, and "the blows and buffets of the world" for which there is no accounting.

With regard to these matters we are powerless. But yet, we cannot bear the thought that there should be problems left which defy our solution, and therefore we assume one. Nor is this merely an emotional reaction to the facts of life; we shrink intellectually from the supposition that the universe should be at such loose ends, so ill constructed, that a part of its implied purpose should be left unrealized. The teleological argument, for which even Kant has a measure of respect, embodies this feeling. The cosmic end, which means the initial purpose of the universe, must find its realization.

But purpose requires a mind in which the intent lodges; it requires an intellect capable of carrying out the design to the point of complete realization. A final purpose, as religion understands it, in the theistic interpretation of that term, requires a mind capable of dealing with matters in a final sense, so that when the mind has finished its operations there are no problems left. All things will have submitted to the supreme will and will be ready to work in cooperation with it toward the final end.

Such a mind must be all-knowing, in order that no circumstance can arise, of whatever nature, with which it cannot deal. This mind must also be all-powerful so that its complete knowledge can be made to function perfectly. Therefore, and not without reason, theism defines God in absolute terms, and it tells us that He is infinite, omniscient, omnipotent, perfect and generally free from all limitations. All this is quite logical, for if the Deity did not possess the qualities named in an absolute sense there would be problems left with which even He could not cope, which would destroy God's absolute usefulness as far as men were concerned. How could we safely leave the direction of our lives in God's hands, if at a given moment He either did not know how to analyze the situation or, having analyzed it, would prove powerless to create a new synthesis of facts which would be more satisfactory. The absolute God in the theistic system is not a mere construction of some speculative mind, but a necessity.

But, granting all this, by conceiving God in absolute terms we have created between Him and men a chasm which it is not possible to bridge. For one who is not bound by time and place, or any form of limitation, is different from those who are thus bound, different not in degree but in kind. Perfection is not imperfection greatly diminished, but an altogether different thing. When the theistic suppositions are brought to their logical conclusion God indeed becomes the "Wholly Other," as both Otto and Barth realized. But the consequences of this fact are fatal to religion because between something and its absolute opposite there are no points of contact. It is in vain that Barth advances the theory that, though there may be no way from man to God, there is nevertheless a way from God to men. This might be so if between the two there existed a relative degree of difference; but when the difference becomes absolute, the path is blocked both ways.

I repeat that in view of the use which theism makes of the God concept it is bound to construct the notion in absolute terms. And yet, by doing this very thing, the concept becomes valueless for the purpose for which it was intended.

But, there are other complications: theism makes God, not man, the norm, the cosmic measuring stick which it uses to determine the value of anything. Perfection is the only positive concept which theism recognizes; whatever deviates from it is negative since it falls below the standard desired. If I insist that a yard is the only measure which, under given circumstances, has a positive value, then I am bound to speak of an inch in negative terms. An inch is something, but it is not a yard, and therefore useless for the purpose which I have in mind to realize.

Since God is the norm, theism is bound to speak of man in negative terms, since he falls short of being God. Man has positive qualities only when you compare him with some other man. Then it is possible to speak of him as more honest, wiser, more efficient; but when you compare him with God, this is impossible. All you can say is that he is not God; and if God be the standard, man must be considered to be a deviation from the standard.

Hence the emphasis in these days is upon this deviation from
the norm. We are being constantly reminded of man's sin, his
helplessness. Gone are the days when reputable theologians
quoted with approval James Freeman Clark's statement of faith:
"I believe in salvation by character and the progress of mankind
onward and upward forever."

"War weariness," some will say. Twenty years from now the
present pessimistic tendencies in theology will prove to have been
but a short lived interruption of the general trend of optimism
which started in the early seventeenth century and which has not
yet reached its peak. Twenty years from now mankind will no
longer be tired; it will have regained its normal strength, and
with it its normal belief in itself.

The argument has much to support it, and it does not require
much prophetic insight to predict that Barth's theological works,
now on display in the reading rooms of the theological seminaries
in order to facilitate constant perusal, will find a much deserved
rest on the shelves of a less frequented part of the library, once
another generation of theologians has grown up.

Nevertheless in point of logic the present generation is perfectly right. If it is a fact that God possesses no limitations, and
if due to this circumstance He is the positive element in the
scheme of things, then for men negative qualities alone are left,
and a pessimistic attitude with regard to them is utterly justified.

But a question starting with "if" is based on a hypothesis, and
a hypothesis is not the same as a theory resting on proved facts.
Where did theism discover this absolute God? In the universe?
Surely not, for whatever we discover there has its limitations.
Even if we argue that the universe is endless, this would only
prove that within its boundlessness there may be discovered, end-
lessly, limited forms of existence. In man? Assuredly not, for
he too is limited. Where then is the discovery made? The answer
fails utterly.

Moreover, how could one hope to discover such a God, where-ever He might be? Man, by reason of his limitations, can know only the finite. Calvin's well known phrase *"Finitum non capax Infiniti"* contains a truth which cannot be denied. Revelation, upon which theism relies, is no help in this matter, for if the absolute God should seek to reveal Himself to us as He really is, our mind would fail to comprehend Him. If, on the other hand, God would try to make concessions to our limited understanding, He would have to take on limits Himself, and therefore would not reveal Himself to us as He really is.

The entire matter remains highly confused. The God concept is introduced to clear up a puzzling situation, but it is so defined by theism that it cannot possibly do this. It never pays to try to solve a problem by the introduction of a new factor, which is itself more of a puzzle than the original perplexing question. The construction of the God concept in Theism is an artificial one. The "Wholly Other" is made responsible for the guidance of the lives of men, which are so different from His own, that to God they too must seem the "Wholly Other." This makes no sense.

Now, since theism uses its artificial idea of God as the one dependable yardstick with which to measure all things, both man and the world in which he lives, being subjected to this incorrect evaluation, become artificial as well. Consequently, when theism comes to deal with man, it makes artificial demands upon him, and condemns him for doing things which, being man, he cannot be expected to escape doing. He is asked to be absolutely obedient to a divine law, constructed without any reference to his own natural desires, or ability to perform. He is asked to accept God's judgment of what is right and wrong, and abandon his own. He is urged to renounce any right to make ultimate decisions, but to leave those to God. He is supposed to have a free will, but he must not use it freely in opposition to the will of God.

In proof of man's weakness, and his utter dependence upon God, it is urged that he is incapable of discovering ultimate answers to ultimate questions, and it is said that he shows his sinful nature when he pretends to have discovered such answers; such a pretense is a sign of pride, the worst sin of all, Niebuhr tells us.

This is a sweeping accusation, and on examination it is found to rest on an insecure foundation. Are there any ultimate problems which require ultimate answers? If there are, and if the answers to them are found, would it not follow that there are no problems left? Should we not then live in a universe in which no one would ask any further questions? That would be death. Has God found an answer to these perplexing difficulties; has He found an answer now? Theism tells us, "Yes." But we discover no evidence of this answer. Difficulties abound among men; and let us not forget that to a God deeply concerned with man, the troubles of His creatures must ultimately be His own. He has not solved them now; that He will ultimately do so is an assumption still in need of proof. We have every reason to ask why God, to whom all power and all knowledge belong, including foreknowledge of what will happen in His creation, why such a God allows a world to come into being in which such difficulties occur. This must be due, either to an act of His will, which would lead to the supposition that perfection deliberately desires imperfection, which is logically inconsistent, or else to a lack of power on the part of God, which would make him limited. This latter possibility is denied by thoroughgoing theists, but not by another group of people, less orthodox in their theism, who count among their number John Stuart Mill and Edgar Brightman.

Humanism objects to an artificial construction of any concept that plays a part in the field of religion, but it resents particularly a false interpretation of the idea of man. Theism pronounces sentence against man for being what he is, imperfect, and for not being what he was never intended to be, perfect. There is no sense in this. Iron is not bad because it is not gold; under certain conditions it is better than gold, that is to say, better fitted for a specific purpose.

It is foolish to condemn a man for not being God, or to think of him as an inferior being for that reason. A dog is not inferior to an elephant because it is less strong; it is merely a different kind of an animal, and it performs a different function. A man performs a different function from a God, should one exist, and the question to ask with regard to both of them is, whether either within the sphere of his specific activity performs that function well. Whether, so far as God is concerned, this question can be answered with an unqualified "yes" is at least a debatable matter.

Humanism admits that as far as men are concerned the question must be answered with "no." Men fall below the level of their maximum moral capacity to perform, both individually and collectively. There exists a great deal of evil that could be avoided and a great deal of possible good which is not being realized. Humanism is greatly concerned about this. It has reason to be, for it denies that man is inherently weak and therefore incapable of correcting these mistakes. It places the responsibility for the existing evil squarely upon man's shoulders, where it belongs, and it is untiring in preaching its gospel of individual and collective righteousness.

But humanism, unlike theism, does not look down upon a man because he has his limitations. It does not require him to perform a task for which, in view of these limitations, he is patently unfit. Humanism does not ask men to become perfect, and to create an order of things in which there will be no further problems, in which there will be no need of choosing between the better and the worse. Equally, humanism knows nothing of ultimate aims, so dear to theism, and it does not censure man for lacking information regarding them. Indeed, it would side with Reinhold Niebuhr in condemning anyone who pretended to possess such knowledge; only it would not call such a man sinful but foolish.

Humanism would never ask that man, for purposes of determining the right and the wrong, should use a yardstick which is not normal to him. It agrees with Protagoras that man is the measure of all things, at least when he is concerned with the evaluation of his own experience. It is useless, and therefore foolish, to use any other measure. In sharp contradiction to Karl Barth's well known teaching, humanism maintains that not God's opinion, but our opinion regarding our life is of supreme importance to us. Granting for the sake of the argument that there is a God who does entertain opinions concerning human affairs, God's opinion becomes important only when it squares with our own experience. Man may be wrong when he tries to examine his life and to evaluate it, but he cannot be set right by merely giving up his own opinion in favor of another, even a better one, until he has given his intellectual assent to it, and has recognized it as right. "He that complies against his will is of his own opinion still," Samuel Butler wrote in his *Hudibras,* and he was not far wrong.

Humanism takes man to be the measure of all things which concern him. Its doctrine is that the seat of authority resides within us, and not outside of us, and that therefore our human judgment is the last court of appeal in all matters touching human life which require to be scrutinized. This does not reduce humanism to subjectivism. Through check and counter check a *communis opinio* can be established which still allows for a measure of individual variation. In mechanics it is taken for granted that it is impossible to grind a part of a machine to the exact size required. A certain degree of tolerance is therefore allowed; and its limits are determined by whether the deviation from the theoretical absolute measurement still allows the machine, to which the part belongs, to function satisfactorily.

A like degree of tolerance may safely be allowed in human thinking. No absolute norm can be set up, but men of common sense and good will can agree on a relative norm. If the variations of opinion are so great that confusion and unhappiness result, we are clearly outside of the limits of allowable tolerance; and we must try to achieve a modification of the diverging opinions. But whenever that is not the case, the fact that people hold individual opinions need not bother us, and indeed should be encouraged. Common sense must decide whether society functions as may be expected, and this is precisely what common sense has been doing throughout the course of history.

Men make errors, very serious ones, but in the long run we may trust both man and the common sense that guides him; were it otherwise there would be no human race at all. We need no superhuman yardstick to give us the right dimensions. If we had one we could not use it. Weights and measures, physical as well as moral, derive from our own needs. When in 1790 the French National Assembly appointed a commission for the sake of determining upon a convenient scientific measure, this group of men in its report of the year 1795 suggested the meter, a ten millionth part of a quadrant of the earth through Paris. The reason was one of convenience, a measuring rod 39.37 inches in length is easy for men to handle. An inhabitant of another planet, ten times at tall as we are, presumably would have chosen a measuring unit ten times as long. Thus in all matters, religion included, we choose what seems to fit our needs. If we are in error the matter will correct itself in time, for with religion as elsewhere the trial and error method yields the only dependable results.

Humanism contends that whoever, in the field of religion, starts his reasoning with God and reasons down to man will not arrive at reliable conclusions, because he uses the inverted, that is, the wrong method; he argues from the less known to the better known. If he is a Barthian, the case is even worse, he then will reason from the unknown, the "Wholly Other," to the known. Such an attempt has never proved to be successful.

Anyone who wishes to be helpful toward the clarification of the religious problem should start by using all the factors which are within his reach, and everyone of those is to be found clearly within the limits of man's life and his experience.

Humanism starts from a frankly human level, both with regard to its religious theory and its practical efforts to make this theory concrete. Does it attempt to reason up to God? The answer fails, because thus far it has not discovered God, surely not the God as defined by theism, no personal God, no God definitely interested in human welfare, no perfect God, no God who is not subject to the limits of time and place. Some room, indeed, might be left for defining the God concept in terms of pantheism; but concerning this matter there is no unanimity of opinion among humanists, although they are surely more friendly toward pantheism than toward theism.

The point is that the religious concern of humanism is not first of all with God, but with man. Religion is definitely a human concern in the sense that it has something to do with setting things right on this earth, and in order to do that it must use the tools which it finds here below. The cure for the illness is where the patient is; it matters little whether we are talking of a physical or a mental illness. The elements which make for health are in the sick body, and we must stimulate them to an increased activity. Unless this can be done, medicine has no value. Theism, which denies that man has adequate power to cure his own ills, since, so it says, no one can pull himself up by his own bootstraps, must look to another source to bring about recovery. It does so, but by defining the nature of that source in absolute terms it has made contact between the physician and the patient impossible. Moreover it has forgotten that in the process of recovery the participation of the patient is of more importance than the medicine of the doctor, and by defining man mostly in negative terms it has rendered such participation impracticable.

Humanism, which maintains that the positive factors in man outnumber by far the negative ones, has not fallen into this error. It is perfectly willing to rely on man's capacity to bring about both his own improvement and the improvement of the world at large. It may do so, because it does not expect the impossible either from the individual man or from society. It is not waiting for the Kingdom of God to descend upon earth. It asks for no greater results than can be secured by one who is subject to the limitations which circumscribe the life of man. But within those limits it demands the maximum obtainable.

Humanism points out that the evil in the world is due not only to the wrong use which we make of the opportunities for constructive action which present themselves, but even more to our neglect to employ all of the chances for right action which are available. Our sins of omission are more than our sins of commission. We are like a carpenter who uses half of his tools and allows the rest to lie idle.

Theism tells us that a reconstruction of the world through human power alone is impossible; but the fact remains that we have used but a small fraction of the means at our disposal toward making the world better, so that we cannot tell what is possible. In the past a country as vast as the United States was thought so unwieldy that it could not continue for any length of time, except under a strict and highly centralized government. But through the establishment of a proper relation between individual freedom and collective responsiblity it has continued for almost one and three quarters centuries. It is, indeed, one of the oldest political structures now existing, in the sense that its form of government does not essentially differ from the one envisaged by the founding fathers.

By the increased and more skillful use of the means at our demand, far greater changes for the good can be brought about in our world than we can imagine. Nor are these changes merely of a material nature; it is wrong to suppose that moral improvement is impossible. Ethics and psychology are not merely descriptive disciplines; they are functional as well, operative in the direction of bringing about better moral and mental conditions.

Practically we all admit this. We establish schools, and support churches, because we think they can build character. We

think of penology no longer in terms of punishment adminis-
tered for the sake of revenge but for the purpose of correction.
We work at improvement all day long; and then, if we are
theists, we deny that real improvement is possible except through
the interference of God. Clearly there is a discrepancy between
theory and practice.

If it should be objected that all this is no more than a relative
improvement limited to worldly affairs, not ultimately significant because the ultimate issues are not touched, humanism
would like to be informed what these ultimate issues are and
whether they are real or mere constructions of the speculative
mind. Even the scholastics agreed that *esse in intellectu* is not the
same as *esse in re*.

Humanism quite willingly admits that man has wider relations which should be studied. He is a part of the universe, and it
is impossible to determine the nature of the part until we know
something of the character of the whole. Any attempt to determine those relations in the widest possible sense humanism
welcomes. Through the study of our wider environment we may
well be forced to change our present opinion concerning ourselves. Humanism, unlike theism, does not say that it has all of
the answers to questions which it is possible to ask concerning
the "nature and destiny of man." It does insist, however, that it
employs the proper method to find such answers, if any are to be
found: the method of trial and error, which, successful in all
other fields of inquiry, is likely to be successful in matters of
religion as well.

IV. The Problem of Sin and Virtue

Any theist of the more pessimistic variety who should chance to read this chapter is sure to venture the remark that the title is twice as long as it should be. There is a problem of sin, undoubtedly, but how can there be a problem of virtue if the substance which gives rise to the problem is lacking?

No one denies that there are different levels of human behavior, with regard to which we may employ the adjectives good and bad, better and worse. Few today would agree with St. Augustine in his assessment of the virtues of the heathen, which he pronounced to be glittering vices. Even those who most sharply oppose man and God to man's detriment, as does Karl Barth, believe in civic righteousness, and by word and precept show that they have faith in it. But all of this does not alter the fact that no virtues can be attributed to man except in a limited, and not quite real, sense. It is not without interest that in the index to Reinhold Niebuhr's *The Nature and Destiny of Man* the word "virtue" is lacking, though the word "good" occurs several times. The reason seems clear; we can employ the notion good with regard to any number of things, situations, and circumstances without inviting criticism, but we use the expression virtue almost exclusively with regard to man, and at this point objections are likely to appear.

Does man possess positive virtues which follow necessarily from the very character of his being? Can we say in other words, "Man, being man, is bound to do good most of the time?" Here is a question to which diametrically opposing answers are constantly being made.

The opposite has often enough been asserted: "Man, being man, is bound to do evil." The "General Confession of Sins," found in the Book of Common Prayer, states positively "that there is no health in us," nor do we find any limiting clause. True, the "Confession" is an ancient statement which no one is expected to take too literally, which is just as well, since few do so take it. But, the church has not changed it; and even those who repeat the Confession with certain mental reservations would be greatly surprised if their minister should ask the congregation to repeat in unison, "We are filled with health."

We have been told so often that we are sinners that we have come to believe it; and so infrequently have we been assured that there is good in us that we hesitate to accept this. To admit one's sins, frequently and sincerely, is counted a Christian virtue; to point to the fact that one is capable of doing good is called self-adoration, and it is claimed that by so doing man makes a God out of himself.

Both Bernard de Mandeville, in the seventeenth century, and Friedrich Nietzsche, in the nineteenth century, pointed out the psychological dangers which follow such a doctrine. When the negative elements in religious teaching predominate over the positive ones, the doctrine becomes useless. Man's natural instincts will assert themselves, his common sense will rebel, and men will drift away from a church which teaches what our instinct tells us cannot be true. This is, in fact, what is happening today.

The whole discussion in this particular field has been vitiated by an arbitrary definition of what is to be understood by virtues and vices, and this was the necessary consequence of the artificial construction of the God-concept to which I alluded in the last chapter.

The first question to be answered is this: "Who determines

the nature of virtue and vice, God or man?" "God," the theist replies; "Man," says the humanist. If God's decision is final in this matter, there is little else for man to do but to accept the verdict. But, since the finite mind cannot understand the infinite one, the reason for this decision will never become clear. This means that we shall be forced to regulate our moral behavior according to a rule which we do not comprehend, and which, to make matters worse, we did not help in establishing.

The consequences of this fact become clearly evident when we study the list of actions which we are prohibited from doing. Even Calvin admitted this. We must not take the name of the Lord in vain. Why not? If we are Jews, we must obey the dietary laws. Why? We must abstain from any work on the Sabbath Day. Why? The reasons are by no means clear. One should scrutinize the whole list of alleged vices and discover plenty which can be so called only because tradition has it that they must be thus considered, not because they reveal any reasons why evil consequences should flow from their practice.

A good many of the so-called vices are mere taboos which have developed for reasons no longer apparent to us and which gradually have been referred back to some decision on the part of God, partly no doubt because in that way they would find a support not easily questioned by the average man. Sometimes this was done deliberately;[1] sometimes it was the result of a gradual development in which no deliberate intent can be detected.

Occasionally taboos conflicted. At the beginning of this century a minister in a Protestant church on the continent of Europe was allowed to smoke and to drink alcoholic beverages within moderation, but he was expected not to dance or to go to the theater. In the United States, at least in the more liberal churches, a minister might dance and go to the theater, but the men in the pews frowned on smoking and drinking. For a person who

---

[1] Compare Robert H. Pfeiffer, *Introduction to the Old Testament*, (Harper, 1941), Chapter 4; I. Benzinger, *Hebraische Archäologie*, p. 276.

served churches both in Europe and in America, it was a matter of some difficulty to get the moral law as affecting a minister straightened out.

But in the same sense in which many of the vices on the official calendar bore no visible relation to any evil consequences which might result from them, many acts officially classified as virtuous could not conceivably lead to an increase in good; in fact, the opposite was more likely to be the case. It was counted a virtue to accept without question what the Bible or the church taught us. Why? Has the Bible ever been proved to be an infallible book? Scarcely. Does it provide us throughout with a uniform doctrine regarding the problems of life, particularly with regard to the so-called ultimate problems? It does not. Has the church never erred; has its doctrine been consistent with itself throughout the last nineteen centuries? He who would answer that question in the affirmative would prove to be a poor church historian.

Why is humility a virtue and pride a sin? Both are deviations from the true norm. A man should strive to have a correct appreciation of what he can and what he cannot do. There is no more virtue in undervaluing oneself than in overvaluing oneself. There is no virtue at all in pronouncing oneself to be utterly powerless to do any good.

It has already been suggested that the artificial construction of the God-concept is at the base of the difficulty with which we are here concerned. An artificial God is sure to be responsible for an artificial system of morals.

A system of morals should stand in proper relation to the persons who are supposed to put it into practice. As a matter of fact, this is seldom so. Laws, moral laws as well, reflect the temper of the lawgiver, but not the temper and seldom the needs of the people to whom the law is to be applied. It is also true that ordinances are apt to be too absolute; they lack elasticity. Obviously this cannot be prevented; it is impossible to establish a general rule for conduct together with a set of subrules governing all possible exceptions. This would be as though one were writing a constitution together with a full set of amendments. Nevertheless, any law which does not have an appreciable relation to the persons for whom it is intended is sure to be ineffective.

God is the author of the moral law. He therefore determines for us what is sin and what virtue. It is clear that the divine law reflects the mind of the lawgiver and not the human mind. If the lawgiver is absolute his requirements will be absolute. No elasticity is to be expected; changes and modifications will not occur; the law is intended for all time.

It is also intended for all men. It is not reasonable to suppose that God's requirements should vary with each individual and relate themselves to his capacity to perform. As previously suggested this would be illogical, for then there would be as many laws as there are individuals, as many "rights" and "wrongs" as there are men. In the same sense in which the human law is supposed to be obeyed by all men alike, and in the same manner, the degree and the nature of obedience which the divine law requires is the same for all men however much they may differ the one from the other.

But since the law reflects the mind of the Divine Lawgiver, and not our own, we can understand it only to the degree to which we comprehend the Divine Mind. If God is indeed the "Wholly Other," or if it is true, as Calvin says, that the finite mind cannot understand the Infinite Mind, God's law will remain a mystery to us. More than a mystery, the wisdom of God will seem foolishness to man. Only they who could enter into the Secret Counsel of God, Calvin's *Arcanum Dei Consilium,* would know why God demanded that we should do certain things and abstain from doing certain others. But no one is admitted to God's Secret Counsel.

Theism, by reason of its first assumption, the existence of an absolute God who at the same time is the Supreme Lawgiver, has always had a hard time to explain the exact nature of the moral code; both sin and virtue are very indefinite concepts in its theology. Theism is constantly telling men that they are sinful, but sin is a deviation from virtue which is the norm, and the norm is given us through a revelation on the part of God. Should you ask however what the precise nature of this revelation is, there is no reply, except a very general one, that it is found in scripture and in the dictates of our conscience. But since scripture is not a unit—and with regard to the moral code contradicts itself at many points—and because the consciences of men often differ radically, the whole situation remains obscure.

If you cannot tell with absolute certainty what virtue is, how, I repeat, are you going to explain sin? Even John Calvin who taught that Scripture was inerrant, and therefore to be taken literally, was forced to admit that the laws found in the Old Testament, which regulated the lives of the Jews, could not be made applicable to modern times, and that therefore only the general moral principles taught in the Bible were valid for all times. This left Calvin ample room for his own interpretation both of virtue and sin.

Humanism maintains that the moral law is not imposed upon us by a superhuman agency, but that it derives from our own experience and that it changes to the same degree to which that experience changes. It agrees with Kant that the law imposed on anyone from above, without his consent and without his understanding of the principles involved, cannot bear fruit in moral action. Moral action is action for a reason both known and approved. It is true, of course, that in the course of our lifetime many ordinances are forced upon us with regard to the formulation of which we have given no direct consent and the import of which we fail to comprehend. The average man, for instance, does not know too much about banking regulations and probably nothing at all about the rules governing city planning, though he is affected by both. But if he lives in a democracy, he has delegated the power to deal with such matters to men who are supposed to be acquainted with the problems. If they err, and the results of their error become apparent, he has the power to recall them and to appoint others in their stead who will act with better judgment. This obviously cannot be done with God. His will is supreme; He need give no reason for his actions, and if He did, we should not be able to understand the reason.

Good and evil are human concepts which bear definite relation to the practical consequences of a given mode of action. Whatever in the long run proves to have desirable consequences, men call good; and whatever results in undesirable consequences, they call evil. We do not start with a general judgment touching a type of behavior the correctness of which we presume will be proved by the consequences, but we look at the consequences of an action first and then formulate a judgment. Whether those consequences shall be called desirable or undesirable is determined in the end by the common sense of the masses, not by abstract speculation. Indeed abstract speculation in many instances does little else except give theoretical support to the practical judgment of the many, a decision which has already become evident in their concrete actions. From the long range practical judgment of the masses, there is no appeal to any higher court, unless it were to an even wider and more prolonged experience of those same masses.

And this is right, for after the same manner in which the lower animals have discovered by experience the things needful to their continued existence, as well as those things which they should avoid, it may be taken for granted that mankind has done the same. If this had not been so, there would have been no human race at the present moment.

When we consider a mode of behavior which makes the continuance of a satisfactory life possible, we call it the moral code whenever we speak of men; when we are talking about the lower animals we use the expression a pattern of behavior. The terms are different, but the meaning is essentially the same. We are trying to say that in either case a certain form of behavior is necessary if life is to be prolonged in a satisfactory manner. The fact that men reflect upon the matter, whereas the animals do not, makes no essential difference. The point to be remembered is that with men, as with animals, rules of behavior are not the result of some law written in the sky, some fixed pattern set by God, but the consequence of a gradual discovery of types of action and thinking which will prove serviceable toward the increase of well being in the widest sense of that term. Whatever functions well in that connection we call good, and whatever functions ill, evil. There is nothing mysterious or superhuman about the matter.

That does not mean that the process is wholly automatic in the sense that we accept without question the things good for us and avoid those things which might cause hurt. If that were so, there would be no moral problem at all. The things which recommend themselves as good have often a hard time being accepted. The consequences of a contemplated action are frequently misconstrued, and then evil follows. The interpretation of our experiences is a slow process or else war, which is definitely an evil, would have been discontinued long ago. It is a question of trial and error, but we are concerned with a *human* trial and *human* errors, and with an outcome, due to *human* activity, which presently will take the form of a rule in which the result of the experiment is embodied. To sin does not mean to break a divine commandment; it means a deliberate action against rules which our experience teaches us must be obeyed if men are to be happy.

In this connection the argument used by Professor Trueblood in support of the divine origin of the moral law seems weak. He acknowledges that the content of the moral law differs as between one nation and another, and indeed as between two individuals. He maintains, however, that the urge itself, the "thou shalt," cannot be explained apart from a superhuman origin. But this idea leads to impossible consequences because a mere urge, apart from its content, obviously can have no value, any more than a mere shape apart from the thing which is being shaped. The urge to kill and maim is often quite as strong as the urge to heal and do good. Are both to be referred back to God merely by reason of the intensity of the stimulus which leads to action?

Theism insists that only God can make the major decisions in the world which He has created. The formulation of the moral law is one of the major decisions. This cannot be left to man since among men there is no unanimity of opinion regarding the ideas of good and bad. Hopeless relativism would be sure to result which would militate against the creation of dependable laws for action. Man may apply the God given law, or not apply it, as he chooses; here a measure of freedom is granted him. But the one who applies the rules and the one who formulates them are not the same person.

Theism is essentially pessimistic with regard to man because it denies him the power to formulate the final rules which shall regulate his behavior. He cannot say, "This is good," or "This is bad," and be ultimately right. When man does this, he is guilty of pride and therefore of sin, since he is attempting to displace the law of God by the law of man.

Because man is doing this constantly and deliberately, he is permanently in a state of error and sin. Hence the theist knows only the problem of sin and not the problem of virtue. Theism is not unaware of the fact that men perform virtuous deeds but they find, thus theists claim, their explanation in the impartation of the grace of God; it is God working through men. Man, not being the true author of his own good actions, these cannot be imputed to him for righteousness. It is different with sin; there according to theism the responsibility lies definitely with us, not with God who, being perfect, cannot be held responsible for it. Theism is constantly impoverishing man to enrich his creator.

Humanism is not pessimistic regarding man, nor indeed optimistic; it endeavors to be realistic. It definitely recognizes the problem of sin; it is quite insistent in asking the question, "Why do men so often act against their own best interests when they know very well what those interests are?"

But humanism recognizes a problem of virtue as well. For it is a problem, not easily dismissed, why the vast majority of men live decent and honorable lives in spite of the manifold temptations to do otherwise. Crime makes the front page because it is the exception rather than the rule. No paper in New York would think of printing the statement that on a given day two million husbands did not kill their wives, and that during the same day no safe was cracked or a house set on fire. People rather expect that these things will not occur, and when their expectations are not fulfilled, they are amazed and feel that comment in the papers is quite in order. A righteous man cannot expect much publicity until his obituary is printed, and not much then if he were so virtuous as to be uninteresting.

When one realizes how relatively recently the human race appeared upon the earth and how many things there are which still puzzle it; when one considers that until the discovery of printing exchange of thought between one nation and another was virtually impossible so that no common effort could be made toward the mental and physical improvement of mankind; when one remembers that the increasing density of the world's population intensifies most of the existing problems, if it were only because of the fact that competition between individual and individual, nation and nation becomes keener, the marvel is not that so many, but that so few, mistakes have been made.

In many instances evil results do not derive from evil intent, but from lack of proper insight or information. When we try to solve an economic problem through the instrument of war, we do a foolish thing which invariably results in disastrous consequences. Yet it is absolutely untrue to say that the millions who participate in the war either wish it or deliberately desire the horrible results which follow upon it. Practically everyone is a victim of the situation which has developed; it is hard, as experience shows abundantly, to place the responsibility where it belongs. To say that war is the result of the essential sinfulness of mankind is to talk nonsense. The vast majority of men prefer peace to strife; and if properly informed and guided, they would wish to continue in peace. War never originates with the masses. They can be made to make war against their own instincts, but it requires a good deal of indoctrination.

As with the masses, so with the individual. The possibility of choosing the worse in the presence of the better is constantly present, yet most people live to the end of their lives without committing flagrant crimes against their neighbors, or indeed without wishing to do so. And if one should argue that the wish to do wrong is always present in every human being, but that public opinion prevents this desire from becoming realized, then one would have to explain how public opinion, a potent force for good, could originate within a group of men who are individually evil.

Humanism does not deny the existence of wrong but it urges again and again that there is more good among men than evil, since no society could exist for untold centuries if its negative qualities outnumbered its positive ones.

For this reason the religious technique which humanism employs differs radically from the one commonly used by theism. Theism is afraid that men will overrate themselves by claiming virtues to which they are not entitled, which idea would make them undertake a task for which they are not suited. Humanism is concerned lest men do not undertake the task for which they are equipped by underrating the inward strength which they possess. Hence the average theistic sermon is sure to contain a warning to the hearers that they are weak, prone to evil, and unable to overcome their weakness and sin by relying upon their own power; they must rather place their trust in God and pray that He may help them out of their present unsatisfactory condition. This does not mean, except in extreme cases, that theism does not expect men to cooperate with God. No one in his right mind would still agree with the opinion of Nicolas von Amsdorf, that not only are men unable to perform good works, but that an attempt to do good deeds imperils their salvation. It does mean, however, that the source of strength is in God and not in man.

The average humanistic sermon reminds men of the fact that they are potentially good and that there is no known reason why they should not actually be so. It tells them that all things in the world, and no doubt outside of it, are equipped with the qualities they need in order to deal with the problems which they are likely to encounter, and that man is no exception to that rule. Men are therefore urged to rely upon their inward strength, which can, and therefore must be used, to an extent far greater than is now the case. Humanists do not teach, as is often said, that men are gods, who can do anything they please. Men do not have to be gods, for their task is not the task of a god. They have a limited work to do, and for the execution of that task they are well prepared. They therefore have the moral obligation to use the qualities which they possess for their own sake and for the sake of others. If they refuse to do so, they are guilty of selfishness which humanism considers the main sin, rather than pride. The next chapter will show the influence of this view upon the ideas of salvation and regeneration.

V. Salvation and Regeneration

THE MAIN PROBLEM with which the Christian Church has concerned itself is that of salvation. The question of regeneration was less important, in a practical sense at least, because the church possessed no means to bring about the change implied in this concept. All it could do was to indicate a certain technique which might be instrumental in bringing about regeneration. Attendance at mass, prayers, confession, the sacraments of baptism, the eucharist, and others would combine, it was hoped, to create a mental disposition friendly toward religious improvement. Whether such improvement would be realized or not, no one save God could say with certainty. One thing was sure, however: the mere possibility that the means of grace placed at our disposal might not be effective gave us no right to dispense with their use, since this would be certain to lead to our perdition; *extra ecclesiam nulla salus.*

Ultimately both salvation and regeneration were in the hands of God. True, the Roman Church allowed for a measure of co-operation on the part of man. He could, by the performance of good works, do his part toward the gaining of ultimate salvation. But, extreme Calvinism denied this; man could lend no help toward his own salvation in any sense, because he could do no good works. Yet, in spite of this undoubted fact, thus Calvinism taught, man was bound to obey the divine law overtly, no matter what the consequences as far as he himself was concerned, for in doing so he paid honor to God which homage is man's chief duty.

It cannot be denied that a considerable change has taken

place in theological thinking regarding this matter since the days of early Calvinism. "Creaturely activity" is encouraged on the whole; good works, far from being "glittering vices," are taken at their face value. It is generally assumed that outward evidence of virtue reflects an inner condition and that good fruits can be borne only by sound trees. With the exception of extreme fundamentalists, few would believe that God holds another view of the matter, and that a good man, for all his seeming goodness, may still be in danger of perdition. Indeed, most men are Universalists; and the idea of hell, so potent in the Middle Ages, has lost its power to frighten. Few ministers, like Jonathan Edwards, would preach today on the fate of "the sinner in the hands of an angry God," since scarcely anyone believes that God is angry by reason of human sins.

But still, the Christian Church has not changed its doctrines of salvation and regeneration to meet the prevailing opinions of the moment. It may be admitted that man is able to cooperate toward his final blessedness; the initiative, it is urged, is not with him but with God. God's grace working in us is the potent factor, not our own will. Our will being weak and our strength inadequate, we stand in constant need of aid and of salvation from the perils which beset us.

In view of this fact it is not surprising that the importance of the second person of the Trinity has grown at the expense of the first person. God as cause may interest the speculative mind, God as support of the moral law may claim the attention of the legal mind, but God the Savior has universal appeal. Speculators and legalists have always been few in number as compared with the thousands to whom religion meant an escape from danger and uncertainty. Those who maintain that God the Son is the true God of the Christian Church, and that the other two persons of the Trinity are of secondary importance, have much to support their contention. It is not without reason that that Christian Church has taken the name which it bears; it calls itself the

Church of Christ rather than the Church of God. And, if anyone should contend that Christ is God after all, the obvious reply would be that by Christ the average man means God in his function of savior; whether or not this happens to be modalism, and therefore a heresy, matters very little to him.

How is salvation to be accomplished? The method is not for us to choose. In the same sense in which the infinite and perfect God determines the nature both of good and evil, He equally decides upon the method of salvation. When we examine the dogmas that bear upon this matter, we have no difficulty in recognizing the period in history in which they originated. They are the product of a time in which the concepts, law and justice, bore a far more arbitrary construction than they do today. The law, in theory at least, was the will of the King: *le roi le veut.* True, the laws were instituted for the welfare of the subjects, but the King determined how that welfare was best served. He equally determined the way in which the law should be enforced. The sharp tripartite division of power into the legislative, the judicial, and the executive which Montesquieu advocated, is not of early origin; it was scarcely discovered, as the French writer supposed, in the forests of Germany.

God makes the laws; man breaks the laws. God determines the method by which man shall be saved from the consequences of his disobedience. In this process man plays a passive part. The Church has never officially accepted Lessing's explanation of God's saving act as one of the education of the human race, of divine instruction through which society and individual men are advanced by slow degrees from a state of passivity to one of activity, thereby becoming increasingly responsible for their own moral condition. On the contrary, God appoints a savior for us and imputes his virtue to us. We pray God to forgive us our sins, not for our own sake but for the sake of what Christ wrought for us.

It may be granted that the doctrine of the Church has lost

much of its crudity. Admittedly the notion of a wrathful God, unwilling to forgive his own children until blood had been shed to satisfy his demands, has become more of a historical curiosity than a true reflection of present belief. Even so the idea that man cannot save himself, that he cannot pull himself out of the mire by his own bootstraps, is still much a part of presentday theological thinking. Man is still counted essentially weak. Why? The reply to this question is that man is expected to do a thing which, being man, he cannot do: to measure up to a theoretical standard of perfection. Precisely what this standard requires from us is not quite clear; in theory no doubt it means perfect obedience to the moral law.

But what does this mean in practice, what is the content of the moral law? Our own ideas regarding the nature of moral activity are changeable, and no two persons agree wholly regarding the character of this standard as set by God. In a general way, all agree, whether theists or humanists, that men are often in error because the consequences of man's actions lead to unhappiness. Yet no one knows the exact degree or character of the error. For one thing, it is not sure whether our errors are the result of misinformation or of evil intent. There are many errors of the mind which cannot be referred back to errors of the heart. But yet, the fact that we err at all the more conservative religions count as weakness since it indicates a lack. Even if this lack were one of information only, they believe that, in view of the deplorable consequences, it is of so serious a nature that men cannot be trusted with the responsibility for their own mental, moral and spiritual improvement. The spiritually and mentally strong make no mistakes; whoever does commit errors exhibits a measure of weakness somewhere. He needs aid. And since all make mistakes, all need aid; hence men cannot live without God. Thus argues theism, whatever its complexion.

An easy but rather arbitrary definition of strength! Experience shows that the strong make more mistakes than the weak because they attempt to do more things with regard to which errors can be made. Surely in secular affairs we do not count errors a sign of weakness. When on December 7, 1903, Wilbur Wright succeeded in lifting his flying machine from the ground, it was a pitifully inadequate contrivance; it would fly but 59 seconds. Everyone knew how little had been accomplished compared with the ultimate theoretical goal; and yet everyone realized how much had been accomplished, for a heavier than air machine had actually flown, a thing which had never happened before in the history of the human race. No one thought of this new invention in terms of lack of accomplishment, but rather in terms of success; the result arrived at was not perfect, but it pointed in the direction of perfection. That was enough. Perfection is not the acme of accomplishment; on the contrary, it is the dead end. It never represents an actual possibility, but only the condition of a human mind which is too tired, too ignorant, or too little venturesome to be able to dream of something beyond the limits of the present accomplishment, and wishes things completed once and for all. And a mind no longer capable of a new dream is very close to the point of mental extinction.

To err is to be active; to be active involves the possibility of error. We can eliminate errors only by becoming more active in the sense that we explore other ways of solving the riddle before us. Why should we suppose that in matters of religion the process should be a different one? Why, in that particular field, should we use standards different from the ones which we customarily employ? Why should we explain the nature of man by taking account of what he lacks rather than by giving thought to what he has achieved? Why should we use the distance between man's present status and perfection as a proper measurement and not the distance between his present status and utter imperfection?

To say that nothing has been accomplished, or ever can be effected, with regard to moral improvement is to fly in the face of facts, and to indulge in a theory which has so little support in reality that no sane person accepts it in his heart. For if anyone did, the logical consequence would be that he would stop any attempt toward the moral improvement of the human race, and not even the more extreme of Fundamentalists would go as far as that. To say that in the eyes of God our attempts in the direction of moral betterment have no significance is to make a statement which cannot well be proved, and it is also to make a reflection upon the efficiency of the alleged author of the human race for creating so poor a piece of handiwork.

And yet, somehow this idea lingers in the official teaching of the churches with regard both to salvation and regeneration. We are constantly warned against pride; we are ever told to remember how narrow the limits of our power are. We live, we are reminded, on borrowed strength; to suppose that we can save ourselves is to suppose the impossible; it is in fact to make a God of oneself.

There is very little difference regarding this matter between the more liberal and the more conservative theistic churches. On the surface there seems to be a significant difference; but when we go into the matter more thoroughly, we find it to be otherwise. Salvation, to the ultraconservative churches, means deliverance from the wrath of God; to the liberal it betokens preservation for a larger life with God. This difference points at a diverging opinion regarding God, but not with respect to man. In either case man needs help because he is too weak to help himself; the ultimate issues, the important part, are in the hands of God. Therefore in either case the process of salvation, as far as man is concerned, is essentially passive.

Salvation should fruit in regeneration. This term occurs but twice in the entire Bible. We find it in Matthew 19:20 and in Titus 3:5. In both cases the word παλιγγενεσία is used; to become new again. In Matthew 19 the conditions surrounding the followers of Jesus are expected to become new when "the Son of Man shall sit upon the throne of His glory"; in Titus 3:5

the change looked for is a moral one. The literature upon the subject is extensive. We meet different opinions regarding the manner in which regeneration is to be brought about. Is baptism essential or is it not? Does regeneration mean that we must first die unto ourselves, surrender our personality and "put on Christ," or do we retain our personality but seek a wholly new objective? Men entertain different ideas on these points.

But one thing is sure: we cannot become new through our own efforts. We are both incapable of becoming different from what we now are, and unwilling to do so. It is characteristic of the "old Adam" that he does not want to change into a "new Adam." Calvin attributed this fact not only to the depravity of the will but equally to the corruption of the intellect. This derives from the fact that we are flesh. To be carnally minded is death. "Grant," says Calvin, "that there is nothing in human nature but flesh, and then extract something good out of it if you can."[1] He quotes 2 Corinthians 4:4, "the God of the world has blinded them that believe not, lest the light of the glorious gospel of Christ, who is the image of God, should shine into them."

With modifications, very considerable modifications indeed, the Calvinistic argument has continued in theism. The stress is no longer on man's evil mind or corrupted intellect; Satan has disappeared from the stage altogether. But, nevertheless, man, because he is man, is not what he should be. Both Rudolf Otto, the liberal, and Barth, the conservative, speak of God as the Wholly Other. This means that God is what man is not, and man is what God is not. God possesses the ultimate standards of truth, and He knows the final answers to all questions. This is so because He is God. Man, because he is man, and the very opposite of God, is wanting in both particulars.

There is therefore something essentially wrong with being man, because it involves a lack of an ultimately dependable standard of truth. It follows that man lacks certainty with regard to

---

[1] *Institutes*, Book II, Chapter 3.

the goal of life; there is a deficiency of directives, which implies
an existence which at no time can be quite sure of itself. A ship
without dependable compass, and a rudder that cannot be trusted,
can hardly be called seaworthy.

Hence a power, not ourselves, must supply a dependable
compass to us, and a rudder that will steer the ship in the right
direction. Even to Kant the Categorical Imperative is not something that belongs to us as men, by the very necessity of our own
being; it comes to us from without, it is something given. In
reality it is nothing else but the voice of God, and it is indeed
used as a proof for the existence of God.

It may be admitted that in modern theism the role which
man plays is not utterly passive. The compass is given to us, but
it is we that must steer by it; the rudder is supplied, but it is our
hand that must manipulate the tiller. But even so, the magnetic
pole is not of our choosing, God is that pole, and therefore all
steering occurs with reference to Him.

The words salvation and regeneration do not figure largely
in the humanistic vocabulary because they do not represent concepts for which humanists find extensive use. "Saved from
what?" "Regenerated into what?" a humanist would ask. Surely
not saved from the wrath of God, for God could scarcely turn
his anger against man because he, His own handiwork, turned
out as poorly as he did. An engineer who constructs a faulty
machine cannot very well blame the machine for being what it
is. If it be urged that a machine has no free will but that a man
has, the humanist would reply that an omnicient God would
know full well in which direction our free will would drive us.

Regeneration into what? Are we such a poor piece of work-
manship that we must give up our proper genus and become
something wholly different from what we now are? Should God
dwell in us, or Christ, rather than that we should inhabit our
own house of life?

Men need to be changed, but scarcely to be saved or to be

made over into something entirely different. Sin is a reality in man's life; this humanism is quite ready to admit. He, who willingly acts against a moral law, the validity of which he himself admits, sins. But no one, not ourselves, can save us from that unfortunate condition, whether God or man. Men can plead with us; they can point out to the noble example of those who made most out of their own lives; but further than that they cannot go. God could give us a new personality, yet that would not be saving the old personality, but killing it and then creating a wholly new one.

Salvation, if it is to have any moral significance at all, implies that through an act of our own will we deliberately forsake a given course of action and substitute another for it, and that we do this because we are convinced that the second course is the better one. It is clear that our opinion may be influenced by the example set by others, because men do nòt live in a vacuum; but the final act is ours, and ours alone. If God should encompass us with a protecting wall, so that temptation could not touch us, He would not have saved us in the sense that He would have made us better men. He only would have prevented us from sinning. When I lock up a would-be murderer in a cell, I prevent him from killing, but I do not take away his desire to kill.

Humanists, therefore, would rather not use the term salvation at all. They prefer to speak of a change which a man should undergo, not in the passive sense of the word but in the active sense. Salvation is brought about whenever we choose to sit in judgment of our selves, pronounce judgment against ourselves, and then act in accordance with that judgment. As a matter of fact, this is what all of us, whether theists or humanists, expect men to do; and when they fail to act according to this expectation, we condemn them. In practice, therefore, the argument that a man cannot pull himself out of the mire by his own bootstraps, but needs the help of God to that end, does not sound very convincing. Surely, if a man committed a crime, and then pled innocent because God had not given him the power to control himself, he would have some difficulty in having his plea accepted, even by a theist judge.

This admittedly "creature activity" does not betoken undue pride on the part of man, as Reinhold Niebuhr tries to prove at such great length in the seventh chapter of *The Nature and Destiny of Man.* Only deranged persons "forget that they are involved in a temporal process and imagine themselves in complete transcendence over history." Or, in other words, only deranged persons forget that they do not have "the final answers," and deny, that, even when sitting in judgment of their own actions, they may use imperfect standards of judgment, . . . which are not necessarily the same as utterly false standards. No one *could* oppose "self-made standards to God's standards," for the good and sufficient reason that no one can tell for certain what God's standards are.

Our innermost instinct, the very law of our being, warns us to trust the standards which are ours for the time being, at least until further experience tells us that there is something wrong with them. And this, incidentally, will not be the case quite so often as Dr. Niebuhr seems inclined to suppose. On the surface men are forced to alter their opinions, true; but the deepest lying reasons why they act and think have not changed much in the course of the centuries, any more than the basic behavior of any living thing below the human level has altered. The ultimate causes for action and thought are too firmly imbedded in the very core of man's being to make essential changes likely; if there were something wrong with them, mankind could not have continued on the face of the earth as long as it has. To suppose that God possesses the masterkey which will fit all locks, and that He has left us with keys that do not fit the locks of the doors which we needs must open is to make an absurd statement because it renders God absurd. If that were the case we should, indeed, be in need of salvation, but salvation from the inept handling of the situation on the part of God.

And what is true of the idea of salvation applies with equal force to that of regeneration, at least if one is to understand by that term more than moral improvement, a wholly new birth. It is human to blame the tools for the wrong use which we make of them, and to assert that if we had only possessed better implements, our work would have turned out better. But that is a poor excuse; a good artist can do marvelous work with very imperfect aids, and a bungler will perform indifferently no matter what implements he uses. Christianity, much more than Judaism which preceded it, has always had a fear of matter and has made it the universal scapegoat for all that went wrong. The Christian Church did not dare to tax God with the responsibility for evil[2] and even hesitated to look for the root of sin in the spiritual half of man's makeup, since that was most akin to God's own nature; therefore our flesh must be blamed. That which was most obviously a part of us was thereby condemned.

Somehow evil, error, sin, illness, and death could not be accepted as a normal part of human existence. Human life it was figured, in order to be perfect, should be without friction. Hence we must be delivered from the flesh, saved from the consequences attendant upon being matter. We are urged to struggle with the flesh, not told to use it for the sake of reaching worthwhile goals. It is counted a liability, it cannot be made into a tool with which the good and the beautiful can be fashioned. Safety is found in becoming spirit. Regeneration involves the loss of the very essentials of manhood, it signifies that we shall become more and more like to a being, God, whose characteristics, as defined in Christian dogma, make Him the very opposite of what we are.

There is something unhealthy in the desire to be essentially different from what we are, and in not accepting the world as it

---

[2] It would have been logical to do so, since God of his own free will created man, knowing beforehand that he would sin.

is. It bespeaks lack of courage, lack of daring, and above all a lack of a sense of the real. A Dutch proverb tells us that we must learn how to row with the oars that we have and not waste our time in longing for something which we manifestly cannot get. When Margaret Fuller said that she was willing to accept the universe, and when Carlyle, hearing of it, remarked that "she had better," both were right. It is all there is, whether we are willing to take it as it is offered to us or not.

Humanism urges us to accept whatever we find ready for our hands to use, and to employ it for the purposes for which it can be made to serve. It asks neither for salvation or regeneration. To be sure it is not satisfied with the results which we have obtained thus far. With the tools which we have at our command we can do much better work than we have been doing. And, it is precisely this fact which should urge us on to make better use of the materials we have.

Why doubt our power to take care of our own affairs without supernatural aid and thus lame our hands? If truly believed in, such a doubt should logically lead to defeatism, surely to an extreme form of passivity, which comes close to defeatism. Why confuse the issue by talking about ultimate answers to human problems which are hidden from us, and present only in the mind of God? Human problems are limited problems and therefore call for limited answers—limited, that is, to the matter under consideration. It is foolish to suppose that before being able to answer a question which presents itself to us, we should first require the power to solve all the riddles of the universe.

And these answers, limited in extent but sufficient for our purpose, men can make and *have made,* as history proves again and again. How often do theists wait for the voice of God to instruct them, before making a decision? How many decisions could they make if they did?

Humanism not only accepts the universe as it is, but within the universe it accepts man as he is. All things existing on the face of the earth are capable of dealing with the problems which legitimately are theirs: man is no exception. We know that all living creatures may be improved in the sense that the possibilities present within them may be changed into actualities; this may also happen in man. But this certainly does not imply a virtual denial of the true worth of his present status. Perfection is no part of humanity; therefore, in order to judge the value of man that standard should not be applied. A horse is no less valuable although it cannot fly. The only question is whether men are capable of performing the tasks which they are intended to perform. That they are capable of doing that, some of the greatest of the human race have proved. If the majority falls short, our task seems clear: it is to change every human potential for good into good actually and truly realized. To carry out the task is within the limits of our power.

VI. Diverging Theories of Value

THEISM BELIEVES that there are values *per se*, the nature of which is determined by God. This obviously must be so because the one who created the universe, and who maintains it in being, must know what is good for it. One may trust an inventor to know more about his invention than anyone else. It is manifestly nonsensical to suppose that a thing becomes worthful only when the people in general fully understand its nature. Not one in ten millions clearly comprehends the intricacies of the vast calculating machines now in use; this does not prevent them from being valuable. The whole world derives benefit from them, even those whose knowledge of mathematics is nonexistent. The only defensible attitude of mind on the part of those who do not understand the problem is one of trust toward the one who does understand it. Someone knows; we participate vicariously in that knowledge. This someone knows both for himself and for us, and in solving the problem he disposes of it even for those who did not know it existed.

God knows; He knows all there is to be known. He not only recognizes the problems of which we are aware but in addition an infinite number of which we have no knowledge at all and which nevertheless demand solution for the sake of men. We must therefore trust Him and accept His explanations which are suited to our limited capacity of understanding. God not only tells us how our problems should be solved; He reveals to us what those problems are. Our own unaided experience does not tell us all we should know about the nature of good and evil, sin and virtue, salvation and regeneration. Even John Calvin admitted that most of the dogmas which the Christian Church teaches bear no relation whatsoever to our normal human experience. If God had not revealed their content to us, we never should have discovered them.

A problem solved means a value gained, and when God informs us with respect to the number of the questions which demand an answer, and in addition provides us with the answers, He supplies us with values from a treasury to which we men have no access. God does not ask us where our interests lie: He tells us what our interests are, at least what they should be. That is the very object of the divine revelation. Those who would substitute exploration for revelation place themselves before an impossible task. "Canst thou by searching find God? Canst thou find out the Almighty unto perfection? It is high as heaven; what canst thou do? Deeper than hell; what canst thou know?"

Since values are permanent, they need a permanent keeper. It follows that they cannot be in the keeping of man who is transient. This is not to be understood in the sense that values are empty abstractions, dissociated from human life. They are, most theists would tell us, eternal ways in which God plans to deal with human lives in order that they may become valuable. In this sense they anticipate human existence as possibilities which become concrete when the occasion demands it. By way of analogy let us suppose the case of a man who discovers an entirely new combination of chemical substances. What the practical results will be he does not know, because the combination, never having existed before, has had no chance to prove how it will act under given conditions. And yet, its effect under all possible circumstances is absolutely predetermined; it will be A rather than B. Nature even now is ready to act with regard to an infinite number of possibilities, although we shall not become aware of the nature of that action until the possibilities have become actualities. There are laws, ways of behavior, which are dormant, but which will assert themselves the very second a chance presents itself for them to become active.

Translating this into terms of religious significance we may say that God is ready to act in a given manner whenever He deems this wise, "in his own good time." But this means that God chooses the moment for action, not we. It is He who controls the means for effective activity, not we. It is He who ultimately introduces value into the situation, not we.

It must not be forgotten, thus theism reasons, that the concept of value from the divine standpoint differs essentially from the one resulting from the human point of view. We, men, are interested in the solution of individual and isolated problems and to bring such a solution to pass becomes for us an end in itself. God, on the other hand, is interested in the collective disposal of all problems, which means that God will not have attained his end until the final problem shall have been mastered. It is upon this very foundation that the teleological argument for the existence of God rests. A condition in which nothing is left to be desired should be the end of all things; only an all-powerful being can create a condition like this; therefore an omnipotent God must exist. Such a situation, once realized, would obviously be both final and permanent: final because there would be nothing left to achieve; permanent because the last problem would not be solved if an element of uncertainty were left.

It is manifest that in the final and permanent solution of events we men can have but a subordinate part, that part namely which God allows us to have. We are needed in the same sense in which a bricklayer is needed to lay bricks in a building which is in process of construction; but we must work according to the plan which is furnished us. If we should alter any detail, the divine architect will call us to account and make us change our work over again in conformity to the original blueprint.

According to Augustinian theology, God is the only true reality; such reality as man possesses is derived, borrowed. The reason for this is that God is His own cause, whereas man is not. God needs no outward support to maintain Himself in being, but man does. Indeed in his instance a continued creative act on the part of God is needed (*creatio continua*) to assure the prolongation of his existence. In a modified form this view is continued in theism. Man "does not have the answers"; he must look for guidance to God even where his everyday affairs are concerned. "Except the Lord build the house they labor in vain that build it; except the Lord keep the city, the watchman waketh but in vain." The relation of man to God is described as that of the subject to the king, or the child to the father. Man does not make his own law; he obeys the law that is imposed on him. As a child he not only respects his father's wishes; he follows them obediently because his own judgment has not ripened.

All this imposes upon us a predominantly passive attitude which militates against the creation of true values on our own responsibility. It even argues against the possibility of discovering true values created by some other power. Only He is able to realize the worth of a thing who knows for what it is intended. Those who do not know the nature of the final goal will be ignorant of the ways in which it can be reached. We shall never know how the ultimate success is gained. True, man may boast partial and limited successes; life is not without its victories; but they do not count in the long run. In fact they stand in the way of obtaining the desired final result. In Freeman's masterful biography of Robert E. Lee, the author repeatedly points to the fact that Lee's lieutenants persisted in trying to gain individual successes, which they often succeeded in doing, but always at the expense of the overall plan. Stuart, and particularly Longstreet, constantly refused to subordinate their individual wishes to those of the one who was responsible for the general strategy and tactics, General Lee. The battle of Gettysburg was lost that way, and it ultimately led to the defeat of the Confederate armies.

Thus by following our own devices we hinder, even though we cannot ultimately prevent, the consummation of the divine plan.

There is but one sensible course which we can take, which is to accept the divine plan as it is presented to us in the belief that it embodies ultimate values which our present state of limited knowledge prevents us from recognizing, but which will become clear to us when God's design shall have been carried to its completion. This means that we are forced to attribute value to something which we do not at present understand, the worth of which we should never be able to comprehend if we were left to our own unaided experience. More than that, it may well be that the very things which God expects us to accept as worthful will appear worthless to us. The wisdom of God may seem foolishness to man.

It may appear that this picture is somewhat overdrawn, but this is not the case; not if one believes that only such things can have true worth as further the ultimate divine plan. It is patent that we, humans, who do not know the character of that plan will be ignorant of the way in which its consummation can be achieved. A trained engineer will know what should be done in order to construct a highly complicated machine. A layman is well advised to leave the matter alone, lest by his ill-guided activity he disrupt the plan which the engineer had in mind to carry out.

Obviously when it comes to ultimates we cannot say, "This is or that is valuable"; we can only pray the Lord to tell us where true values are found in the humble conviction that He knows and that we do not.

It is interesting in this conection to study both the Apostolic and the Nicene Creeds. It may be taken for granted that neither instrument represents in toto the fundamental religious convictions of most of the laymen and clergymen in present day Christian churches; but the fact remains that these creeds have not been officially abolished and that in many churches they are repeated by the congregation on suitable occasions. In a number of churches, notably the Danish Lutheran Church, the Apostolicum is still the text of orthodoxy, so that, to put it mildly, the clauses contained in it must contain a sufficient modicum of truth to justify the retention of the whole.

As far as the Apostolic Creed is concerned, it is noteworthy that, apart from one historical reference to the crucifixion of Jesus under Pontius Pilate, and an allusion to the Holy Catholic Church, not one single clause is supported by the type of historical evidence which is ultimately referable to sense experience. A belief in God as the maker of heaven and earth, in the virgin birth, in Christ's presence in heaven at the right hand of God, and in His return to earth for the purpose of judging both the quick and the dead, rests wholly on authority; that is, on a willingness to believe without proof. And the same thing is true with regard to the factual existence of the Holy Ghost, the certainty of the forgiveness of sins, and the resurrection of the body. Quite the same, but with added emphasis, can be said with regard to the Nicene Creed.

If it is necessary to believe these things for the sake of our salvation, or even simply in order to get a correct notion of the way in which God proceeds to effect that salvation, each creedal clause represents a definite value, but it is a value handed down to us by God without reference to anything that our experience might lead us to consider valuable. In this connection it is worthy of comment that in neither creed is any allusion found to that which we men think supremely important, moral action. This is all the more amazing in view of the fact that both in the Jewish law and the teachings of Jesus, the main emphasis is a moral one. The point is that there is a great deal of difference between the simple kind of theism represented in certain types of Jewish thought, and in the teachings of Jesus, and the abstract notions which developed in the Christian Church under gnostic influence. Neither the fourth chapter of the Prophecies of Micah, nor the Sermon on the Mount, draw the sharp line of demarcation between God and man which is customarily drawn by the theistic theologians of the present time.

In the dialogue which occurs in Micah's famous chapter there is no question of an ultimate solution of problems in a manner incomprehensible to the human mind, and which stands in sharp opposition to the limited conclusions at which men arrive. Men and God reason together on the same level and use arguments valid for both parties. There is a question of justice and mercy in the sense in which men understand those terms, of walking humbly with God and not of awe before the "Wholly Other" of which Rudolf Otto wrote. In the parable of the Prodigal Son we meet the same situation. If the father represents God and the son erring humanity, both meet on the same level, the human level; all problems are solved in a manner entirely comprehensible to man. The values represented in the tale are moral values in the human sense of this word; moral action is demanded. No law is imposed upon us from above; the divine commands are consistent with our own experience and therefore take on a measure of validity which is not open to doubt.

Briefly recapitulating the argument set forth in the preceding pages, we conclude that theism defines a value as something which God believes to be vitally important for men, whether they themselves recognize its worth or not. The situation is analogous to the case of a physician who prescribes medicine to cure an illness. The patient for whom it is intended takes the medicine because he trusts the doctor, although he may know neither its name nor understand the manner in which it acts.

Humanists do not agree with this theory of value. First of all, it begs the question, because it assumes the existence of a personal God who is capable of dispensing values, which is the very matter of dispute. Secondly, in matters of religion a value is more than something which may or may not prove to have merit in the long run, whether we understand its nature or not. On the contrary, the merit of anything within human life depends directly upon the present understanding of its character and function. An unrecognized value is a contradiction in terms. The medicine which the doctor prescribes, the name and function of which we may not know, does not become a thing of worth to us until it has cured our illness. We may not know the how, but we do know the effect; we have recovered.

If humanists could agree that in the relation God-man God is the active and man the passive element, God the actor and man the one who is acted upon, the situation might be different. But, in that case, it would be impossible to speak of values where man was concerned. It is scarcely valuable to a pawn on a chess board to be moved to another square, even if through this change of position the game is won for the side to which the pawn belongs.

Humanism maintains that self-activity is the very essence of manhood. The creation of values is the supreme form of activity. In matters of religion, where values count supremely, man himself must take the initiative, not some power outside of him; or else the creation of values, at least as far as man is concerned, is by that very fact impossible. It may be admitted that many factors, not of man's making, play a part in the process. But this does not render man passive; on the contrary it gives him the supreme chance for asserting himself. In the same sense in which a sculptor needs matter in order that he may express himself, man needs the world in which he lives. It serves him as raw material which has substance but no form. Substance no man can create; it is in fact "the given"; but the form men must supply, and it is in giving form that primary values are created. Rembrandt's Nightwatch is more than five pounds of paint spread on a few square feet of canvas. It is indeed paint spread on canvas, but in such a way that the material substance disappears and beauty is brought into being. That is Rembrandt's doing; through him paint and canvas are changed into values.

Man is the seat of authority, and he uses that authority to

determine the worth of anything with which he comes into contact. He is scarcely infallible in his judgment; the very thing which at a given moment he assesses highest may prove in time to have no value at all. *Errare humanum est.* But the important thing to discover is whether in the long run, as applied to a great variety of cases, human judgment as to worth is more likely to be right than wrong. Humanism thinks that it is more likely to be right since it is inconceivable that the human race could have continued if the opposite were true.

But, even if we should grant, for the sake of the argument, that mankind continues to make wrong guesses, God's interference would not change the matter for the better. The greatest gift which God could bestow upon us would have no meaning at all until the true character of the gifts were realized by the recipient. And this would still make him the final authority in this matter, for the recognition of a value involves an assent on our part and the basis of this assent can be nothing else but the recognition that the matter to be judged with regard to its worth corresponds to the standard which we ourselves have set up concerning the right or the true or the beautiful.

It would seem that such doctrine, if carried to extremes, would leave room for personal standards only, which would reduce all thinking to a state of hopeless relativism. But there is no reason whatsoever why we should carry the doctrine to an extreme. Indeed, our daily experience should keep us from doing such a thing, since it gives us constant proof of the fact that men, in spite of differences, have much in common, surely enough to make life within the group possible. There are, we know, a few rules of thought and conduct to which all men must adhere if they wish to exist at all, in the same sense in which all human bodies, though differing in many respects, function in sufficiently similar ways to warrant the existence of a science of medicine. There is no such thing as absolute relativism, for this would mean that two men would react against the same environments in utterly different ways, from which it would follow that they had no points of contact whatsoever. We have no evidence of such a condition; diversity and unity are not incompatible. They become that only when we interpret the meaning of these two concepts in an absolute sense. This life never does.

Humanism ,which believes that man is the creator of values within his own life, does not fear that society will disintegrate on account of the different conceptions of value which exist among men. If this could be the case, disintegration would have set in long ago. It is true that in human society we witness a constant friction between opposing ideas, but this could scarcely be called disintegration. Quite the reverse it true: all movement, and therefore all life, depends upon friction. Only death is frictionless. If God, in order to obviate friction, should step in to force His notion of values upon all men, thereby eliminating all differences among them, He would have reduced living beings to lifeless objects.

A favorite argument which theists employ to prove the need for the existence of a God, rests on the assumption that values need eternal support, and that only a being free from the limitations of time and space can provide this. Man lives but a few years and when he has gone, most of what he has tried to accomplish goes with him. And what is true of the individual holds to an even greater extent with regard to humanity as a whole. A day will come when no men will be living on this globe. This would mean that, when the last man has gone, the entire heritage of the ages would have gone with him. This thought is insupportable to theism; Jesus and Buddha, Plato and Kant, Raphael and Velasquez would have lived and worked to no purpose; and with them millions of others whose names are forgotten but who, each in his sphere, produced values worth saving from obliteration.

This argument, though often used, cannot stand the test of rigid investigation. It presupposes first of all that men through their activity create values which continue to exist after their death in a detached manner and which may be appropriated by following generations. Together they would form a *Thesaurus Virtutum* like the *Thesaurus Meritorum* of the Roman Church, an inexhaustible source of values ever at the disposal of the needy.

As a matter of fact, men have done no such thing; what they have done is to leave the record of their life for anyone to examine; they have also through their activity changed certain concrete situations and conditions. Whether this change constitutes a value or not depends upon the reaction of posterity to the change involved. There are some who believe that any modification of Christian belief as it was known in the Apostolic Age means a decrease in value; there are others who hold that modifications are constantly needed. Values are no immaterial entities, they are always concrete, always attached to a thing, a condition, or a person.

Nor need we suppose that duration plays a part in this matter in the sense that whatever continued longest is by that very token the most valuable. Worth is determined by whether a thing fits conditions at a specific moment in history; if it continues beyond that point, its value ceases and may change into its opposite. Most religious dogmas were valuable at the time when they were introduced because then they constituted an answer to a need. When the dogmas were retained after the need had gone, they became a drag upon progress. A note in a musical composition does not gain value because it is prolonged for half an hour, but because it is stopped at the proper moment. Anyone whose automobile horn was ever stuck should feel the force of this argument. There is no need of a God to give eternal support to values, which by their very essence are related to single moments in a human life.

It is obvious that the difference in the theories of values set forth in this chapter determines in the end the difference in general conceptions of religion entertained by humanists and theists. The theists construct their religious theory with reference to what seems most desirable, the humanists with regard to what is possible. The theists have to introduce unknown, or at least uncertain, elements in order to complete the picture; the humanists operate with what they have.

A good deal depends upon what one desires, a complete solution of all problems, both present and future, or an arrangement of the present situation in a manner as satisfactory as conditions will allow, in the hope that future puzzling questions will yield to the same treatment when the time will have arrived to deal with them.

The two programs differ widely in scope, the one takes in time and eternity, the other a fraction of time. *"Qui trop embrasse mal étreint"*; whoever tries to put his arms around a larger load than he can hold will find everything slip from his grasp. Religion is no exception. Values are found in the here and now; they are attached to things we can handle and which we therefore can make valuable for our purposes.

The ultimate end of theism and humanism is the same, the full understanding of all that can be understood. The purposes differ. The theist desires complete knowledge mainly because through it he may learn to understand the ways of God, the humanist because it will enable him to control the things the nature of which he has come to know. To a theist whatever God regulates turns into values; to a humanist, whatever yields to human guidance.

The way of the humanist is hard and long. He can make no extravagant promises, and surely no hasty ones. To most questions put to him his answer must be, "I don't know," or "I do not know as yet." This is disappointing indeed. But his method of approach provides one advantage which the theist does not share with him: when he, the humanist, is able to say, "I do know," he can prove it.

PART TWO

I. Theism and Humanism: Some Preliminary Observations

THE QUESTION to be discussed can be interpreted in a number of ways. Perhaps it would be well to consider briefly what several of these interpretations are and which of them will be followed in this part of the discussion.

Taken one way, the question is simply unanswerable. That is, suppose it is taken to ask what in fact the religion of the future will be. But no finite mind can know the determinate detail of the future (if indeed the future can be said to have any such detail), and therefore the question in this form is not worth further consideration.

The question may also be interpreted thus: are there any indications that humanism is the coming thing in the line of religion, that its power over contemporary minds and imaginations is so clearly expanding that a sound prediction could be made about its future dominance? This is a question for opinion-tasters and sociologists, and we may cheerfully leave it with them, with the understanding that the success of the creed would by no means be an indication of its truth or all-around soundness.

At least for the time being, then, we shall avoid asking what is going to happen to humanism or to a civilization that embraces it as its essential creed. The question is, rather, *should* humanism be the religion of the future, or, to put it somewhat differently, is humanism the religion which should henceforth receive the adherence of reasonable people? Suppose that an affirmative answer is given to this question. Then we should want to know why humanism should triumph. And the answer to that question must certainly seem very simple to anyone who believes in humanism: humanism is true and since we ought to live by the truth, we should believe in humanism. Or again it might be said that even though it is impossible to prove humanism true (some people profess that nothing important can be *proved*) it would be a good thing to believe in anyway, because a better case can be made out for it than can be made out for anything else, and because certain beneficial and positive results will follow from its acceptance.

So far it would seem that we might all agree upon one thing: the primacy of truth. The truth, all right-thinking persons declare, should prevail. Among other things this means that where truth and mere usefulness can be distinguished, our actions and hopes should be predicated upon truth rather than upon utility or expediency. (To believe that the truth should prevail is probably also to believe that in the long run the truth will also be most productive of good.) For instance, suppose that there were an absolutely reliable way of ascertaining the reality of hell (that is, before or without going there). For many of us there would be very little comfort or usefulness in this information, either here or hereafter. But if hell really exists, if propositions asserting its existence are true, he is a fool who denies its existence simply on the grounds that the denial is a more comforting and inspiring belief. Belief in hell might very well convert decent persons into hellions and cast an abysmally morbid pall upon the spirits of many others. But to make the most of ourselves we must acknowledge *what is,* however it bruises us.

To discover *what is,* to apprehend the truth about the reality to which we must conform or which we may hope to mold to our purposes, is much more, however, than "knowing the facts." The "real world" is encountered not merely in sense experience; it is encountered and grappled with by mind and will. Accordingly, to know what the world is with which we must deal, what truth is that should prevail, require reflection, judgment, interpretation of fact, and the venture of the will into concrete activities.

The clash of theism with humanism is not a clash between "facts" (though frequently a clash occurs between theories of how the world is known), but between theories concerning the nature of the world as a whole and of man's place in it. The supporters of either theory need have no greater admiration or abhorrence for the "facts" than the supporters of the other. Ignorance of essential facts or perverse indifference towards such, where it can be proved, is a most damaging blight upon either theory. And neither theory requires a less rigorous concern for fact, for the whole of experience, than the other.[1]

The procedure in the presentation of theism has been controlled by the conviction that the reader wants primarily to have a positive case put before him—he wants to know what theism claims and what reasons can be advanced for these claims. This expectation is essentially sound and should, if possible, be met. Theism cannot really be demonstrated by discrediting humanism, any more than humanism can be established by discrediting and embarrassing the case for theism,[2] for while humanism and theism cannot both be true (so that if one is true the other is

---

[1] Professor Auer seems to suppose that theism has generally recognized and emphasized the "subjective" factors of experience to the loss of appreciation for the "facts." This judgment is not only unacceptable because it is part of a naive sensationalism, but also for the following reasons: (a) he has neglected to show that theism is impossible without this disbalance; (b) he seems not to be aware of the fact that this distinction between "fact" and "subjective factor" is ruinous to his whole case for human values. Thus he fails to show that theism *cannot* look all the facts in the face, and that humanism *can* look all the facts in the face and have any "value" left.

[2] Probably for several reasons, humanism is made out frequently by humanists themselves as primarily a case against theism. For one thing, theism has long been a kind of "majority opinion" in Western religious philosophy, and the humanist may well feel that his first concern must be to clear the ground of this monumental error. But whatever the reasons, the result is unfortunate, because a sound—or even an interesting—ethico-religious program cannot be built upon a largely negative argument.

false) it is at least conceivable that both are false.[3] Hence neither can be proved true by proving the other false.

Some tentative definitions may now be in order.

A religion may be theistic, but theism is not a proper designation for a religion. Theism is a metaphysical theory, that is, a theory concerning the nature of reality, a view of the significance of human life in relation to the total scheme of things. A person could hold theistic convictions and not be a Christian in the full sense, or be a particularly interested participant in an organized religious activity.

Religion includes vastly more than metaphysical theories; and, indeed, in some religions (e.g. Judaism) metaphysical theories are relatively undeveloped and are relegated to the lower places of importance, if not ignored. Emotion, aspiration, value, conduct, indeed the whole fabric and process of life are absorbed into and colored by religion. It can therefore be said that religion is more than one interest or concern among others, for as we see it in its highest forms it is a comprehensive concern. It is more than one attitude toward life and the world: it is a comprehensive organization of life's resources to cope with the challenges of the world and to achieve the fruition of human potentialities in communion with whatever in the world makes for good. In Christianity this attitude is expressed in part by the elaboration of a systematic metaphysic and systematic ethic. That metaphysic is theistic, and that is why Christianity is called theistic.

What, then, is the metaphysical theory called theism? Theism is the theory that the world (including man) is the product or

---

[3] There are in fact several other alternatives: (1) God exists but is non-personal (e.g., The Absolute); (2) God exists, is personal, but is not pledged to the conservation and enhancement of human values; (3) no God exists, and human values are meaningless; (4) no God exists but human values are eternally significant because the soul is inherently eternal. Whether or not these alternatives have been seriously defended and elaborated (most of them have, actually), their existence as mere possibilities is sufficient to unseat any simple program of proving either theism or humanism right by proving the other wrong.

effect of the activity of God, who is personal so far as intelligence, will and love can be attributed to Him, and who governs or directs the world for the realization of the greatest ultimate good, and who has adequate resources for the realization of this aim. Any religion might be said to be theistic which affirmed these things. Thus Judaism is theistic, as is Christianity, and there are elements of theism in Indian religion (*cf*. Rudolf Otto, *Mysticism East and West*) and in the philosophy of Plato. Theism therefore cannot be identified completely or essentially with the Christian faith. Moreover while Christianity is theistic, there is a great deal of Christian teaching that does not logically follow from the prime tenets of theism (*cf*. Chapter IV). For these reasons there is nothing except confusion to be gained by trying to make Christianity and theism interchangeable.[4]

What is humanism? Is it a religion (in the sense discussed above)? Is it a metaphysical theory, or is it an ethical theory? Even though humanism may be presented as the religion of and for the future, it seems to me quite clear that it is not understood even by the humanists as being a "substantive" or systematic and organic religion. But then is humanism a metaphysic? Apparently not in the sense in which theism is, because, a) while the humanist professes interest in the "framework" in which human values are set, he seems to have no unambiguous conviction (if Professor Auer's case is representative) as to what that framework is or even as to how the framework is related to the rest of the picture; b) humanism seems bent upon the adoption of a method which denies any significance to metaphysical questions. And so humanism is left as an ethic, as a conviction about human values and what we should do about them (what kind of conviction

---

[4] There is even less to be gained by the identification of theism with one variety of Christian thought, such as Calvinism. I am proceeding on the supposition that Professor Auer has done this for some other reason than to take Christian thought at what he may suppose is its weakest expression. I do not believe that Calvinism is really cut out for the role of "straw man" in which he casts it; but that is another question.

can be learned from Professor Auer.) Now ethics is part of religion, not the whole of it. The humanist program, accordingly, is to replace religion, and specifically theistic Christianity, with a part or fragment of religion.

Even a noble fragment of religion, however, is in the end unacceptable and unproductive without some kind of a metaphysical base. Is this present debate, then, between a metaphysics on one side and an ethics on the other? No, because the ethical correlates of that metaphysics are not at every significant point hostile to humanism. We shall have to suppose that the debate is primarily metaphysical, i.e., is there a case for theism or is there a better case for non-theism (of which there are several varieties of opinions)? If the latter should be true we should have then to see what particular kind of non-theism made the most sense, and what implications for the good life were involved in it. Professor Auer obviously believes that there is a better case for non-theism than for theism; but he does not tell us what this is, nor how the good life is related to it.

The issue is primarily, though not exclusively, metaphysical. If Christianity rests upon a false metaphysic, upon a mistaken apprehension of *what is,* then Christianity should be revised or abandoned. And if humanism, as a fragment of religion, rests upon a false or incurably ambiguous metaphysics, then it should be abandoned as a reasonable and productive substitute for theistic Christianity. Let us now see why this must be the case.

Every religion is concerned with salvation. What man has to be saved from, what in man is worth saving, how salvation is attained, are questions upon which the widest possible variety of views is held. Humanism, for example, teaches that men need to be saved from ignorance and its offspring, including man's self-destruction. Christianity also teaches that men need to be saved from ignorance ("The truth shall make you free") and all its fruit, but above all man needs to be saved from the life of self-alienation from God and his true good and therefore saved from ultimate self-frustration. But any scheme of salvation presupposes certain things about the universe and about man's place in it. If these propositions are wrong, the proffered hope of salvation is hollow, if not silly. If there is no hell, no one should spend much time working out a way for avoiding it; if heaven be but a dream, the sooner we awake to stern reality the better. No one in his senses will worry about Divine Judgment or hope for eternal fellowship with God, if God does not exist.

Metaphysics, as the working-out of such presuppositions, is, accordingly, indispensible to the adequate development of religion and to any significant ethical fragment of religion. This does not mean that every religious person and every seriously ethical one must be a professional metaphysician. It does mean that every reasonable religious person will seek the warrantable satisfaction of believing that his faith deals intelligibly with the ultimate questions.

Metaphysics is the intellectual foundation of religion, and theism is that foundation for Christianity. It is not the whole of religion; and it is rarely, if ever, the most vivid and the most persuasive aspect of religion. The more vivid elements, the decisive concrete wisdom, the soaring poetry, the commemorative acts, etc., may be the effects of a fuller apprehension of God than reason owns; but theism, as metaphysics, is obligated to stick by frugal and oftimes tedious and plain reason. The theistic metaphysician, on the other hand, is not obliged to cease believing in revelation or to elevate the bare sketches of his science above the more compelling testimonies of the religious life. Yet the rules and the aims of his calling block effectively any appeal to such testimony as constituting proof or evidence admissible to the bar of philosophic reason. Hence, even if he believes that the full meaning of the Christian faith cannot be understood philosophically, he is compelled so far as he is a philosopher to forego any appeal to supernaturally-guaranteed truth. If there is truth "beyond reason," he must not base his argument upon it; neither can he reasonably hope to demonstrate logically the existence of such truth.

It is expected that the humanist will play by the same rules. If there is a case for some kind of non-theism he will state it as fairly and as clearly as he knows how. He will not suppose that the recital of all the private and public mischief *religion* has worked will either prove that theism as metaphysic is false or that his own variety of non-theism is true as metaphysic. In other words, he will try to prove the non-existence of God or the existence of a God different from that of theism; he will prove the unreality of cosmic purpose, and the mortality and transiency of the human spirit and of its dearest aspirations. And just as the theist cannot rightly appeal to the supernatural wisdom imbedded in the traditions of the Church, so the humanist cannot rightly appeal to what every right-thinking modern person knows. Both must suppose that the truth is something more than the high-water mark of opinion, however popular and however expert. Both must suppose that when the ultimate questions have arisen, mere guess-work is not enough, because the religious interest is in life under maximum conditions, and the satisfaction of this interest requires more than surmise.

II. The Central Elements of Theism

In this chapter the fundamental elements of theism will be stated and analyzed. There is little point in trying to make out a case for theism until the principal features of that position have been outlined. Then if one believes theism is to be rejected, he will know at least what it is he is rejecting; and, on the other hand, if he finds theism tenable, he will know what he is letting himself in for.

Theism is, first of all, a theory about God. It is not necessary to suppose that putting it this way implies the existence or reality of God, even if some Christian thinkers have asserted that (*cf.* p. 122). One may have a theory about water-nymphs and mermaids without (unfortunately) implying the concrete existence of such entities; and there is no obvious reason why the same does not hold for God. Atheism is also a theory about God, and the atheist would object vigorously if someone inferred the real existence of God from his denial of same.

Traditional theism[1] offers as its most general "definition" of God the following: God is that being than which nothing greater can be conceived.[2] This definition is designed to express several things at the outset, namely, that God is absolute and that he is perfect.

---

[1] Traditional theism may be distinguished from revisionary theism as follows: the former consists largely of the re-statement and defense of Scholastic metaphysics, particularly as it is found in Thomas Aquinas. Revisionary theism affirms some of the traditional notions but expresses them in non-Aristotelian philosophic modes; and it disagrees pointedly with traditional theism on such matters as divine omnipotence, absoluteness and eternity, and upon the problem of evil.

[2] Anselm's formulation, but one widely accepted by traditional theists.

It is a common conviction among religious people that deity is absolute being. This means that in his own line, whatever that may be, God is unsurpassable. There is no other being that approaches him in power. Everything else waits upon him; he is the servant, the "thing" of none.

What is back of the conviction of the absoluteness of God? For one thing there is the perception that any being less than absolute would be unworthy of worship and obedience. Worship and unqualified loyalty belong only to the "Unsurpassable," for anything less than that would be an ungodly God—one whose decisions and actions might be subject to something still higher up. Such a being might arouse the sympathy of mortal man, for he too knows what it is to be frustrated by higher-ups, but such a God could not elicit unqualified respect or reverence. Moreover, a non-absolute God cannot account for what needs to be accounted for, *including himself.* The "average Christian" believes that God is First Cause or Ultimate Ground—He is what is needed to account for the existence and behavior of the universe. As such God himself is uncaused, underived, which is to say, absolute. If he were not absolute, he would be a cosmic function rather than the cause of the world as a whole—something other than himself would be the reason for his existence, and then this "something other than himself" would be God. And thus, at the popular level still, we are thrust back upon the assertion of God's absoluteness.

The initial definition also concerned perfection. For many this term has the connotation of value, in addition to mere power, and certainly the initial definition (God as that being than which nothing greater can be conceived) is congenial to that connotation.

Ordinarily perfection is attributed to much besides God. In common discourse something is perfect if it is everything it should be, if it lacks nothing that properly pertains to it. A perfect blueberry pie is one that leaves nothing further to be asked of blueberry pie. And so far, a perfect God is one that lacks nothing that properly belongs to such a being, that is, to an unsurpassable and underived being. Whatever power and value pertain to such a being, he has or is. He may lack something, e.g., yellow or edibility, but these do not pertain to his kind of being, that is, to the highest possible degree of spiritual being.[3] And as absolute, all power and all value pertain to him, which is to say, the power and the value of everything else are surpassed by the power and value of God.

(It might be well to note in passing that "all power and all value" is inherently ambiguous. I have not hesitated arbitrarily to assign the meaning given above because theism, as distinguished from the garden variety of pantheism, cannot consistently suppose that every instance of power and of value is literally God.)

Christian theologians are sometimes tempted at this point to say that God is *really* perfect and that everything else is radically defective. Professor Auer takes this to be standard theism, but in this I believe he is quite mistaken, as I shall hope presently to show.

For theism the perfection of God means that God's being has a completeness and inclusiveness not to be attributed to anything else nor to the sum total of things other than God. It is important thus to take "completeness" and "inclusiveness" together, because many other things are complete so far as they go. The botanist may say of a jonquil, "Here is a perfect specimen." Presumably this means that, no matter how many more jonquils you might bring in, none would fit any better into the "definition" of jonquil, none would meet the specifications any more completely. Yet this perfect specimen does leave something to be desired: it cannot satisfy every expectation that jonquils, and

---

[3] Theism teaches that God is spiritual or immaterial substance. The assumption is that spiritual being in any degree is higher than materiality. To think, to feel, to will, are all activities richer and greater than material substance boasts.

The traditional theist would not permit the phrase, "highest possible degree of spiritual being" because he believes that God is not in the same scale of being as the creatures are. God is beyond the scale of being, the degrees of being. This is his own way of underlining the absoluteness of God.

flowers in general, quicken in us. It cannot exhibit all the color variations and nuances that the whole species can; and it cannot exhibit all the wonderful variety of shapes and delicacies of patterns that the whole range of flora contains. Nor are these things said in disparagement of the "perfect jonquil": let all its beauty and perfection be admired. But the realities of the situation ought not to go unnoticed. It is particularly to be noted that its perfection is bound up with *exclusiveness:* for it to be that jonquil and nothing else it must rule out an infinity of other possibilities. And this is the fate of every finite thing, and may indeed be an important part of what is meant by the word "finite."

On the other hand, according to theism, God is both complete and inclusive. His value ("goodness," "beauty," etc.) expresses without qualification or exclusiveness whatever is of value anywhere, and His being expresses what everything else strives for and exhibits under limited mode or degree. And therefore the following formula emerges: in order to be or to affirm itself, the finite *rules out* an infinity of other possibilities; whereas the existence of God is the affirmation, the *ruling in* of all significant possibilities.[4]

Theism teaches that God is personal. He acts as only spiritual being can act; that is, he thinks, he wills, he knows, he loves. This does not mean that God is a big man in the sky. Such terms as intelligence, will, love, purpose, can be and must be carefully and critically predicated of deity. It is true that theism is sometimes accused of uncritical and reckless anthropomorphism, and there is no doubt that some theistic religions are occasionally so interpreted by devout and uncritical souls. Yet theism as a

---

[4] So, in medieval theological traditions even the Devil is permitted to exist. If he were *absolutely* evil, he would be non-existent. Here the analogy is that of the parasite that cannot live unless the host lives. Evil is a parasitic growth upon existence and being. Thus the Devil's situation is acutely embarrassing for himself, because he is the supreme instance of self-contradiction: for him to exist at all is for good to triumph over evil. Therefore he hates himself without stint.

whole is free from this vice of "reckless and uncritical anthropomorphism" (a vice in metaphysics, though frequently a shining virtue in poetry and in practical piety). The instrument of its freedom from such defect is historically the theory of analogy of being and of thought. According to this theory certain notions are correctly thought in relation to God *provided they are thought non-literally*. Thus God is spirit, but he is not spirit subject to the conditions in which we know spirit in ourselves, i.e., as dependent upon physiological functions. God exists, but his existence is not qualified by space and time[5] as ours is. And so also of personality and self-hood. To be human is but one way of being personal, of being a rational spirit. While it is necessary to think of other and vastly greater spiritual beings as analogous to ourselves, if we are to conceive of such at all, it is not necessary to suppose that to be human exhausts the possibilities of spirituality. If it be retorted that we can make no sensible statement about such higher spirits because we do not experience them directly, the theist replies that significant theoretic knowledge of them is still possible. Such being can be conceived even though it cannot be properly imagined (represented by images drawn from experience). And all that is at stake for the moment is whether such being is a possibility.

In summary of the theistic conception of God, it has been noted that God is a personal individual, self-identical, absolute, and supremely perfect. God is not the universe or nature. The universe is not a rational, personal individual, but it is the creation or expression of just such a being. God is in the world, which is to say that the world is known to him and is penetrated by his love and directed by his wisdom. But, again, God is not the world, and the world is not God.

What is the theistic interpretation of the world (the uni-

---

[5] Even when theists argue that God is in time or is intimately concerned with time, they agree that God's knowledge of time and his ability to deal with it far surpass our knowledge and ability.

verse)? Everything that is not God is created or produced by
God and is directed (in one way or another) in its activity by
God. Hence between God and the world there is an irreducible
difference: God is self-dependent and is his own explanation,
and the world is dependent upon God and is therefore not its
own explanation and does not set its own aim. This is the philosophical meaning of the mysterious Christian teaching that God
is "wholly other."[6] God is infinite being; the world is finite being.

In ordinary usage "finitude" and "mortality" are virtually
synonymous. Something is finite if it has a stateable terminus
beyond which it does not exist. This is not the theistic understanding of finitude. A being might be immortal (whether by
virtue of its original nature or through "miracle") and nonetheless be finite, for *finite* expresses its limited, exclusive and, we
now add, its dependent character. The nature of anything finite
is thrust upon it, and in its activity it is radically and continuously dependent upon the cooperation of the environment and
ultimately of the universe. While it always possesses value so far
as it exists at all (and this holds for wicked men and malignant
viruses), it rules out other possibilities; it *negates* other values.
This negation is bound up with its dependency in this way: the
sustaining environment and universe will support it in one line
of activity and not in an other, in the pursuit of certain goals
and not in the pursuit of others. Thus the finite is master of its
world only to a limited degree. If it were absolute master, it
would be God, that is, the pursuit of its own aims would at the
same time be the fulfillment of all other positive aims.[7]

---

[6]Professor Auer is correct in contending that if God were *wholly* other we
should not be able to say anything intelligible about Him, not even that he is
wholly other! We might still have to deal with Him (or It) but we would have
no idea concerning Him that could be known to be either true or false.

[7] We may note in passing the significance of the love of the finite for God.
To love God is to affirm the value of his being. In the Christian faith this is
also to love the world, and particularly, our fellow-creatures, because God Himself affirms the whole, His interest and concern are all-inclusive. Thus *The First
Epistle of John:* "If any one says, 'I love God' and hates his brother, he is a liar."

In the theistic perspective the world as a whole is finite, it is continuously dependent upon God. This does not deny that the universe is an incredibly complex and vast organization or system. It does claim that complexity of itself does not solve the problem of finitude. A complex organization still requires explanation; and the wonderful interlacing of the parts of the universe does not account either for itself or for the existence of the parts themselves.

The theist does not assert that finitude is "bad,"[8] or evil. To the contrary all that God has created is initially good, not simply because he has created it but because "the more being the better," which in a loose way might be said to be the divine motive in creation. God in creation has gone out for the maximum realization of good, for the realization of the widest possible range of potentialities. Since this is the case, and since God is what he is, the world is perfect in its way. It too has what rightly pertains to it, and there is nothing more that could properly be asked of a creation.

Although it is somewhat beside the point, it is interesting and perhaps instructive to observe the survival of this theistic conviction concerning the world in a non-theistic setting. Professor Auer asserts that everything that exists has whatever is necessary for its existence, else it simply would not be at all. It is true that he, along with the humanists in general, is concerned with ridding us of any lingering notion that *human* existence is somehow far

---

[8] There are traditions in Christian theology which very nearly, if not altogether, identify evil with finitude itself, but so far as I can see none of these traditions derives this conviction from theism as metaphysic.

(4:20. Revised Standard Version).

There may be other ways of achieving the ideal universality of ethical aim that the greatest of the moralists and moral philosophers have dreamed of. Surely one of the greatest problems here is the two-fold one of achieving genuine universality (love of mankind) without loss of sensitivity towards concrete particularity (love of *this* person). It is the Christian and theistic conviction that ethical respect for persons and for personality makes the fullest sense only in a world which is ultimately directed as a whole towards the fulfillment of personal values.

below what it really ought to be, but he is willing to risk the wider and implicitly metaphysical judgment that things in general are what they ought to be. Taken at its face value, that is, as he formulates it, this hardly says more than that whatever exists is able to exist. No one will deny that, but either something more than meets the eye is contained in the judgment, or it is not worth making at all. That something more seems to be that so far as a thing exists at all, it is perfect, that is, ready and equipped to exist as just that particular thing; and, he clearly supposes, it is good that it should exist as that particular thing. Again, this latter judgment is made explicitly only of man, but it should be extended to everything else, otherwise the humanist will have to account for the special favors shown man by nature or the universe. Thus where the theist says that God can do no wrong and can make no mistakes, the humanist says that nature or the universe can make no mistakes. But the logic is really different. We can speak of "mistake," in respect to the existence of something if we mean either simply a mistake from our human point of view (which is hardly more than to say that this something displeases or irritates us), or that a power other than ourselves was aiming to do one thing and for some reason actually did something else, perhaps something that should not have been done under any circumstance. For instance, there are certainly times when we say spontaneously that the bed-bug (*Cimex lectularius* where formal introductions are in order) is a mistake. We don't mean that he lacks something, or is not quite fitted out to get along in this world. We mean either that it is a mistake to get into bed with him, or that God (if you are a theist) or nature (if you are a humanist) slipped up somehow—was aiming at something else (perhaps an insect that would clean mattresses) and didn't have the material at hand to do the job right, or turned it over to an assistant who botched the job. But the theist alone can think intelligibly of a power other than ourselves *aiming* to produce an effect and failing to do what was aimed at. Most theists, to be sure, would entertain only with the greatest reluctance the notion that God could fail to fulfill his aim, but in the theistic perspective such an eventuality can at least be meaningfully considered. The situation is quite different with humanism. The humanist is left with the sole alternative, when he says that nature makes no mistakes, of meaning that nature cannot be judged by ethical, rational standards. And if this is so, then nature cannot be indicted either for failure, for nature *aims* at nothing in particular. Only man aims; and this creature, the humanist avows, is withal the child of nature.

According to theism man is a part of creation. He is in the world not as an alien living in dreadful exile from his native land beyond time and space and all things material and mortal but as one kind of created being, with his own perfections and potentialities, living among the other creatures in organic relatedness with them.

Yet the theistic viewpoint also embraces the belief that man is a creature of significant and far-reaching distinctions. These distinctions may be summarized in the terms, "rational spirit" and "person." The possession of reason marks man off from all the other creatures directly known to him, and it opens the way to a kind of communion with God that the other creatures do not have, for the other creatures (that is, lower than man) are caught up in a purposeful pattern they do not comprehend while man's life is profoundly colored by his comprehension of purpose and by his direct participation in purposeful activity. Reason is also a clue to the distinctive organization of life and spirit suggested by the terms "person" and "self." Man is more than a complex organism. He is a complex organism endowed with the power of self-awareness, self-direction and self-evaluation, and these all involve mind and rationality. He is not merely a bundle of appetites, a system of habits and reflexes. He is also a *will*— a unique power for the synthesis of appetite, habit, etc. into a unique pattern of unified, purposeful activity.

Now to call this creature a child of nature is a poetic pleas-
antry, more honoring the parent than the child. Theism neither
denies nor minimizes man's kinship with "all things else created," but it does call attention to the uniqueness of personal
existence; and theists frequently claim that this unique being
is the richest clue to the nature of God Himself.

The humanist interpretation of man—if we may go by what
Professor Auer tells us—reveals a desire to play both ends against
the middle. The humanist affirms the worth of human life in very
strong terms. He is out for the perfection of human possibilities
(except in moments of despair, of somber *Weltschmerz,* when he
says of human values, "this isn't much but it is all there is and
after us nothing"; but Professor Auer would probably read a
despairing humanist out of the church). But the humanist also
affirms the unbroken solidarity of man with nature. Man is a complex organism and is to be explained in terms that apply to all
organisms. Man's sense of having superior value or worth would
seem then to be mere conceit. Being a person entails no unique and
irreducible value, or if it does these values are ultimately mysterious excrescences upon a value-less nature. But surely this metaphysic, if that it is, accords very poorly with the humanistic ethic.
Why should a man feel any greater obligation for other men
than he does for other organisms, say the mollusks? The egoist
can answer this: attention to the interests of other men will get
him more happiness—or whatever else he is after—than attention
to the interests of the mollusks. Humanism, however, generally
repudiates egoistic ethical theories, though I cannot make out
from Professor Auer on what grounds.

The uniqueness of the human situation must be further
understood, according to theism, as *freedom.*

Freedom is a slippery word all-round, and the theists are not
in perfect agreement among themselves on what freedom is
and how much of it man has. Yet it is necessary to arrive at some
sort of rudimentary conception of freedom upon which general

agreement in the theistic cause at least can be obtained. For this purpose it is suggested that to be free is to be able to make out a course that is one's own and to pursue it on one's own power. In slightly more formal terms, freedom is choice of ends or goals and self direction towards them. One's own course need not (indeed *cannot* in the universe in which we live) exclude the courses of others. The point is, the pattern into which *I* fit *their* aims and interests is *my* pattern and subject to my revision and the object of my pursuit.[9] Again, the energy I use in the pursuit of my goals is "mine" by the leave of the universe and of God, but I use it for my ends. My desires and aspirations are superimposed upon a physical-chemical system which obeys "natural" laws but which submits also, within limits, to my direction.

Theism conceives God's relation to this freedom in the following pattern. First, God alone is perfectly or wholly free. He alone is able to make out a course, to set an aim, without acknowledging external and arbitrary limitations; and He alone is able to pursue that course wholly on His own power. Hence again at this point God and man are essentially different. Man's ability to make out a proper course is limited both by external circumstances and by internal factors, such as lack of knowledge, force of habit, etc.; and he is clearly not able to pursue his course entirely on his own power. The success of his plans requires the consent and cooperation of an indeterminably large number of other agents and processes.[10] Second, these limitations upon man's freedom are understood and willed by God as part of His

---

[9] This is very far from meaning that the patterns are fixed and static and are determined without primary reference to others.

[10] In Christian systematic theology one generally encounters in one form or another the belief that man's freedom has also been fatally compromised by sin. There is no inherent contradiction between this belief and the view outlined above, but theism as a metaphysic is certainly not logically compelled to accept that notion, whereas it is compelled logically to reject any notion that corrupts or contradicts the fundamental principle of the freedom of rational spirit in man. Thus even if by virtue of the fall, the will is not what it used to be, it is still free in relation to other finite causes or agents; it is not their prey or their tool.

own plan or pattern.[11] For man is a creature, and his freedom is consonant with creaturely (dependent) existence. Yet man has a greater freedom than any other creature he encounters, not merely because, unlike them, he is able to know the causal structure of nature to which his activity is conformed[12] but also because he is able to transcend this causal network in significant degree. He is never an "unmoved mover," an underived cause, but he is sometimes a prime mover. The will is a causal agent that is capable of dominating (i.e., imposing its own pattern upon) all other relevant causal factors in the pursuit of its aims. Thus man is able both to take the world up into his own pattern, to conform himself to that known world and to the mysterious forces that swirl through it, and to modify that world significantly through his own agency. This agency, theism maintains, is no function or effect of the world or of nature. It derives inexplicably from God.

---

[11] Thus God wills both man's freedom and its limitations, that is its natural or native limitations. The philosophical understanding must resist seduction by mythological and poetic fancies masquerading as metaphysical principles. There is, for example, the *Genesis* story of how Jehovah places restrictions upon the primal parent, for otherwise Adam would master the secret of deiform existence. Action from jealousy or an equally ignoble passion, such as vindictiveness, cannot be reconciled with the root convictions of theism. Plato, among the theistic philosophers, and the Hebrew prophets, from the side of historically-grounded religious faith, both grasped this.

But why then the limitations upon existence in and for freedom? If there is to be creation at all, it must involve limitation of being, reduction or "contraction" of the scope and perfection of being in the creation. God cannot create being equal in perfection to Himself, for that would be the same as the duplication of himself, which is impossible. Creation is the divine self-expression or self-communication through a medium other than His own sbustance. *Cf.* Dorothy Sayers', *The Mind of the Maker,* for a very interesting development of this thesis.

[12] Naturalism, which seems to me to be the metaphysic behind much of Professor Auer's position, sees freedom as no more than knowledge of the causal structure into which every finite agent is irresistably and irrevocably geared. That conception of freedom, and such modifications of it as Dewey and Hegel have made, seem very much like saying that one is free when one knows that he is being run down by a ten ton truck and that the activities of the truck, as of oneself, are parts of an all-inclusive network of nature (or of reason).

Let us summarize the theistic interpretation of freedom. Man is bound to his condition; he is determined by God to be a free agent.[13] And he cannot abdicate this dignity. If he accepts "unfreedom," he does so freely; and while he may contradict himself in this way, the contradiction does not efface his fundamental nature which is existence in and for freedom.

Theism claims that the universe as a whole is the expression of the beneficent mind and will of the Infinite. God created the world on purpose, as he created man-in-freedom on purpose. This purpose, this all-encompassing aim cannot be thwarted because there is no other being with power and ingenuity sufficient to frustrate the divine intent. (It would be pointless to say "wisdom enough to frustrate God's program," since by definition wisdom is the ground of the world, the mind back of it, and cannot therefore be opposed to the world. Hence, if the Devil exists, he is fiendishly cunning, not wise: his "wisdom" is an awful perversion of real wisdom.)

This claim is the sticking-point in theism for most people, the point at which they feel the widest possible gap between theism and the plain facts of everyday life. It seems impossible, or if possible, pointless to accommodate the existence of a world steeped in suffering and frustration with the existence of a supremely beneficent and powerful God. And in the course of the long history of theism many answers to this problem have been proposed. It is impossible to investigate or even to state all those answers here. Rather the hope must be to state the minimal consensus in theistic thought, which is the framework within which the more specific and ambitious answers are given.

The theistic view is that the reality of evil is not incompatible

---

[13] There is no standard theory in theism relative to the way in which the divine will directs, pervades, superintends, etc. the will of the finite. Yet every significant variety of theism teaches that the mode of God's participation in finite rational activity differs radically from his determination of non-personal activities. If a system of Christian theology cannot allow this distinction, it cannot be accepted as theistic (and could it then still be called Christian?).

with the existence of a benevolent and ultimately triumphant God. Evil exists or occurs within a cosmic pattern, a universal order which itself is perfect because it provides for the maximum variety of being and value compatible with real order. But what is this evil within the order or design that does not corrupt the order itself? Ultimately evil falls into two broad categories: (1) pain, (2) sin or moral evil. The occurrence of (1) is no blot upon the universal order, for even if pain, as we experience it, generally results in loss of happiness or the sense of well-being, it does not for that reason result in the actual diminution of being. Indeed, some are willing to contend that pain is a necessary correlate of the higher potentialities of life and spirit; that is, as sensitivity increases with the increase of range of interests and capacities, the possibilities of suffering are also increased. The higher forms of life have a much greater range of feeling than the lower forms, and therefore they undergo greater pain; the human spirit lives by hope and by high resolve and by deep and tender affections, and these can all be blasted, with suffering too great to be borne as the consequence. But we do not know why this should be the case, if indeed there is any hard necessity in it. We do not know why the increase in sensitivity should have to be attended by greater evil, by greater pain. But it is so; and its being so, the theist believes, is not incompatible with a universal order the purpose of which is the greatest possible realization of good.

But what of (2)? Wickedness seems to be just that violation of the universal order which the theist believes impossible, for it seeks to destroy life and order; or, more accurately perhaps, the wicked man wills the destruction of life and value that will not conform to his narrow and limited pattern or order.[14]

---

[14] For instance: the sin of adultery involves the will to destroy the rightful mate of the party of the second part, not necessarily (though God knows frequently enough) in the sense of murdering him or her, as David does in the vivid Old Testament story of David, Bathsheba, Uriah, and Joab, but at least in the sense of blotting out for the time being the efficacy—the "life"—of the

Theism agrees that the partial aim of wickedness is just that violation, but claims that the universal order is actually impervious to that assault. An order that actually caved in where the unrighteous attacked it would in effect be one in which *unrighteousness* could not occur, simply because where no inclusive pattern exists it is impossible to will the primacy of an exclusive and limited pattern over an inclusive one.[15] In such a situation one could will only to impose his will, his pattern and aim, upon other particular patterns and aims (somewhat like Hobbes' conception of the state of nature in human affairs). But this is not in fact what the wicked man does. His will calls in question a whole scheme of things, a whole scale of values.

The whole scheme of things that wickedness defies includes freedom; the freedom, among other things, to defy that order, because an order that provides genuine freedom allows unavoidably for the misuse, the perversion of freedom. A person can make a bad choice; a person's character can become vicious and deeply corrupt through his free choices. But these facts do not impair the soundness of the comprehensive order in which that bad choice is made and that vicious character develops. The order does not make that choice, nor the God behind it and in it. The order supplies the opportunity in which to make the choice; and since the choice, when it issues in concrete activity, is also

---

[15] This analysis assumes that some things are really right, others really wrong, or, in other words, that right and wrong are not simply what is useful and what is harmful for society.

---

image and the right of the lawful mate. The "ideal" Uriah resists inclusion into the pattern of the adulterous David, whether the "real" Uriah would have gladly surrendered his beautiful wife to his lord and king or not. Therefore the ideal Uriah, the efficacious image of Uriah, must be destroyed: the conscience, upon which this image would normally register, must be deadened; the self must be turned over to the powerful thrust of passion, for the time being. Obviously David made no distinction between the real Uriah and the ideal Uriah. He acted to dispose of Uriah altogether. But long before David's sly and murderous schemes had taken Uriah off, he had killed him in his mind. (Society, of course, acts only against the murderers of bodies.)

taken up and woven not merely into the character of the chooser but also into the whole scheme of things, it is possible to say that the universal order places limitations upon choices which are themselves the embodiments or reflections of past choices. Yet these are *limitations,* not inescapable causes; they are framework, the partial definition of the boundaries of the field in which the person must live and choose; but they are not the decisive agency by which he is moved.

Theism maintains that God is not the source of moral evil. This conviction has been expressed in different ways. Plato seems to have wondered whether wickedness might not have sprung from a source totally unlike God, perhaps from a demonic power of some sort. At any rate he is certain that God, the perfectly good, could not have been the cause of evil. Augustine sees moral evil or sin springing from the human will, not from the divine; and so also Calvin and Jonathan Edwards. The traditional theists affirm that God knows "from eternity" that men will sin, but they insist that nothing *makes* man sin, since sin is the perverse employment of man's essential freedom, and without freedom there would be no sin. And all theists believe that God is able to cope with evil in its moral aspects, whatever its source.

God's coping with evil is part of the inclusive pattern of His relationships with the world and His activity in behalf of the world. This pattern and this activity are covered by the doctrine of providence, to which we now turn.

This term, providence, signifies the continuous and effective concern of God for the world, which concern is the expression of God's love. Concern in this context does not mean anxiety. God is not anxious about the world, as though everything had or could go wrong with it. Concern means involvement with and sympathy for the world. Sympathy, again, does not mean commiseration, i.e., inefficacious sorrow over the hard lot of another. For theism the divine sympathy means rather the penetration of deity into the life of the creature, the sharing of that life, the creative and redemptive participation in its aspirations and its frustrations. This is just to say that he who sympathizes with another identifies himself ethically and perhaps emotionally with the other. So also of God. God's providence is not to be thought of as the making of arbitrary, static, and impersonal arrangements for the finite, but as a concern or solicitude that permeates and environs the finite. If this is so, it would be impossible to say of any one benevolent and productive aspect of the world, "*this* is providence" in any other sense than that this particular aspect of the divine activity is a symbol for the whole pattern, the inclusive system, of God's concern for the world.

There is little agreement among theists on how far metaphysics can go in the description of God's love for the world and of His making Himself available for the enhancement of the value of the world and the redemption of man. There is little agreement among them on the matter of whether God's concern for the world takes the form of "miracles," of unpredictable "interventions" in the natural order in the form of particular and special acts of redemptive love.[16]

There is however a fairly wide uniformity among the theists on the question of what provision is made for man who, by reason of his distinctive nature would seem to have a special claim upon divine love. For one thing theism embraces as a cardinal thesis the conviction that the universal order, the divine, cosmic plan, is pledged to the production and enrichment of personality.

---

[16]Roman Catholic metaphysicians believe in miracles, but they also believe that the human mind is unable to comprehend their specific rationality. Hence as metaphysicians they do not introduce the concept of miracle into theism. There are other theists who use the term "miracle" in a greatly attenuated sense: the supervention of a higher form of being, e.g., personality, upon a lower order, is "miraculous"; it cannot be explained in terms of the lower and simpler. But in general theists have had hardly more than a desultory interest in the question of miracle since the 18th century. This attitude of relative indifference is partly justified by the fact that theism as a whole neither stands nor falls with the intelligibility of the belief in miracle.

This purpose and pledge are in and of the "natural grain" of the universe, and therefore human values are no accidental achievement of nature: they are in the works "from the beginning."

As we have noted, theism does not deny that it is possible for rational finite spirits to "go against the grain," and this is not possible to any lower form of existence (in theological language, only man is a sinner). Indeed, the worst afflictions of human existence are the results of going against the grain. The pangs of bodily ills, the exquisite hurt of bereavement, the pallid and the frightful fears that paralyze us are all grievously hard to bear. Still, more dreadful than any one of these or all of them in concert, are the "sins of the spirit," the abominations conceived by cruelty, the pestilences arising from avarice, the nightmarish and desperately enervating fantasies bred by bestiality and prurience. These are the rot in the heart of a man and in the heart of a civilization, the end-state of which is a living death, the loss of real power and the blindness to real value.

All of these ills derive from man's unique gift: they flow from his freedom as rational spirit. Man can and does choose freely to go against the grain.

The cosmic order both tolerates and refuses to tolerate this perversion of freedom, this affront to creative order: and in this paradox is embedded our destiny. Just as any moral order, say a human society, tolerates its own contravention, so the cosmic providential order tolerates its contradiction. Every human society has a law against murder, however wide the variations in its definition; but in every society murder is always a possibility and is always being perpetrated, for every society exhibits values and creates situations which are an inducement to murder. Every society has some kind of sexual code, and in every society this code is violated, because every society creates situations and holds out the possibility of certain satisfactions that are an inducement to the violation of the sexual code. Yet society always refuses to tolerate the assault on its moral structure; every society fights back at the person who goes against its grain, punishing the offender in multiple ways, and making him fight himself and punish himself. In all this there is a reflection of the cosmic moral order, but the analogy must be taken with several far-reaching qualifications. For one thing the cosmic divine order is ultimately and perfectly personal; whereas every human society lapses—perhaps necessarily—into a fateful impersonality both in its rewards and its punishments. This is true of even the most advanced societies, for there too we discover a host of factors other than personal worth deciding what honors, benefits and opportunities a member of that society shall enjoy.

Moreover the basic pattern of the universal order is not retaliation, mere retribution or vindictiveness. It knows nothing of mechanical compensation,[17] precisely because its ultimate intent is moral and personal. Therefore it provides the occasion for the renewal of moral effort, for learning from experience, for the fresh start. It is, in a word, the realm of freedom. Such a realm is a "chancy" one, in which a person may fail again and again to do what he ought and what he might. But the growth of moral character seems inconceivable in any other spiritual environment.

In this chapter we have considered some of the principal claims of theism and have seen how theism addresses itself to some of the deepest and most persistent problems that perplex human life. It should be clear that certain theistic convictions could, with but little modification, be adjusted to quite a different perspective. It is part of the theist's task to show that such convictions can be more productively entertained if the system as a whole is entertained as true. In other words, he ought to show

---

[17] Nothing could be farther from the theistic perspective than the notion (frequently associated with Buddhism) of a non-personal moral order, an order that mechanically hands out retributory punishments, perfectly proportioned to the wrong committed. Such a conception is a systematic denial of the flowering of the human spirit in love that seeks a justice far greater than mere calculation of desert.

that human values and human freedom appear in their widest significance only when these "facts" are related to the existence of God, because God is the absolute center of the theistic perspective.

III. *The Existence of God*

The proof of a metaphysical theory is a very different matter from the verification of a fact-claim. As a case of the latter, suppose I say that the table upon which I am writing is hard. If you wish to discover whether that claim is true, you feel the table for yourself; and if its surface is sufficiently resistant to the touch, you agree that it is hard. This kind of verification is a simple and relatively direct affair, however complex and confusing its presuppositions may be, because it concerns stable features of a "public" and common world. It concerns aspects of the world accessible to all interested parties.[1] But the verification of a metaphysical claim is not so simple and direct. The materialist does not say, "anybody can tell that the world is nothing but physical substance by just looking for himself." The metaphysician does not report the facts in so simple a manner. He theorizes about the facts, he interprets the facts, and he appeals to the facts as evidence for the truth of his theories.[2] The metaphysician tries to set the facts in a framework of theory designed

---

[1] It will not really do to identify "fact" with such easily accessible features of a common world. Fact is also used in relation to the "subjective," private world. I say, for instance, "it is a fact that yesterday I loathed the macaroni set before me." I was the only one who knew that feeling at the time, yet that feeling really characterized a part of the world. You know about it simply because I choose to tell you: I remembered my manners just in time and gave no outward sign of displeasure or discomfort.

[2] I do not intend to make a rigid distinction between "fact" and "interpretation." Every "fact" is richer than a bare report of sensation or of some broader awareness. The interpretive function of mind enters the process of cognition so early and so far down in experience that the separation of sensation from judgment or interpretation can be made only abstractly and applied only arbitrarily.

to embrace them all, that is to say, designed to give a coherent and practically significant view of the world we know and are compelled to live in.

There are many such views, many such systematic theories. Each has its enthusiastic followers who refute all the competing systems and claim the truth for their own. How, in such a hubbub of assertion and denial, of proof and refutation, could the truth be recognized? The situation is not, however, so hopeless as it looks. Those who agree that metaphysics is significant should also be able to agree on how metaphysical theories are to be tested. And one of the things that such people are pretty generally agreed on is that one of the tests is coherence or internal consistency. Another is clarity; and yet another is fruitfulness in and for concrete activity, or for life as a whole. The last element is very important, and for a simple reason: if metaphysics is the attempt to produce a view of the meaning of life as a whole, it ought to make a real difference in living, it ought not to be the kind of theory that makes no ripple upon the waters of concrete existence.[3]

It should hardly need saying that there is no neat yardstick for the determination of the adequate or decisive degree of any of these requirements of a metaphysical theory or for the way in which they should be combined. Because such a measure is lacking, the durable systems have been revised over and over to meet the thrust of searching criticism and to synthesize fresh discoveries about the world. From this it seems a natural inference that such theories are really born for conflict with one another and that in this conflict the relative truth and concrete significance of the various alternatives are worked out. Here the poet

---

[3] It will perhaps be noted that the test of "economy" has been overlooked. Well, it does have a subsidiary significance, but that is all. Metaphysics in the first place is concerned with generalizations of the widest degree; and in the discipline it is axiomatic that no more of these shall be formulated than is strictly necessary. . . . Mere tidiness, both in the housekeeper and the metaphysician, can easily be over-rated.

and the metaphysical philosopher seem to part company. The philosopher does not try to enthrall the imagination with a beautiful and stirring vision. He has a theory about the meaning of life and the world; and he hopes, by fairly pedestrian ways, to establish the truth of this theory. He seeks to show that his theory, properly expressed and properly understood, should elicit the assent of the mind. To prove such a theory is to show that it takes hold of the world better than any other theory does; and to prove in this way is back of the formal procedures—the syllogisms etc.—which are part of the tools of the trade of metaphysics.

It was said above that metaphysical theories seem born for conflict. This can be seen also in the fact that to prove such a theory involves disproving its rivals. Fundamentally there are two ways of accomplishing this latter objective. One is to show that the alternatives of the favored system are really unthinkable; that is, they cannot be thought without falling into absurdities. This is called dialectic. It is a method that has no more than incidental significance at best for "scientific thought," where the primary objective is to account for a limited range of facts and where several theories may do this equally successfully at a given time. But the scientific theory does not have to account for itself, it does not have to show how it can be held, while the metaphysical theory is legitimately held to give this accounting. It must show how the theory itself—and the mind behind it—are possible if the world is what the theory asserts it to be. Thus the scientist does not hesitate to accept the atomic theory of matter simply because the theory does not account for the activity we call theorizing. That theory is not cut out for so broad and general a purpose as that. On the other hand, suppose a philosopher proclaims that the world is devoid of meaning, of any meaning at all. If this theory is true, his theory itself has no meaning, but if the theory is false, at least the statement that it is false has meaning; and so taken either way, the theory cannot account for itself. Or again, take the extreme formulations of behavioristic doctrine which denied the existence of consciousness. If consciousness does not exist, then I cannot be aware of (conscious of) the statement that consciousness does not exist; and, even worse, he who makes the statement cannot be aware of it either; and therefore, if the statement is true (if indeed on that theory truth can properly be talked about at all), there is no reason whatever for supposing that its truth or its falsity can ever be *known,* since knowledge is obviously a function of consciousness.

The use of dialectic is determined by the basic conviction that a genuinely significant theory must be as free as possible from internal contradiction. This is perhaps a kind of rudimentary rationalism, for the philosopher believes that an utterly self-contradictory notion *cannot* be true, *cannot* really be faithful to reality.But all philosophers do not agree on the converse, viz., that a self-consistent theory must be true, must hold good for the "real world." Those who reject the converse believe that something more than self-consistency is required of a metaphysical theory before we can admit its truth. And this "something more" is always some kind of an appeal to the actually experienced world.

The second way of disproving or refuting a metaphysical theory is to show that it ignores or misinterprets certain essential facts. Every durable type of metaphysics of course tries to get in all these essential facts; it tries to account for the "full orb" of human experience and the environment in which it is set. And therefore the charge of ignoring significant aspects of experience is not quite so simple as it sounds when it is preferred against such a theory. What the criticism generally signifies is that the full flavor, the solid impact, of a range of experience are not discernible in that system. The system blanches the richness of certain areas of experience and leaves it but a faint shadow of the original.

This method of refuting a system reverts rather frequently

and easily to dialectic. The full significance of the criticism that "facts" are being ignored or are being given the once over lightly is that if those facts were taken seriously the theory would have to be revised, for the admission of the full significance of those data would split the theory down the middle.

The aim, then, of a philosophical proof is to leave but one pair of alternatives relative to that proof: accept it or be convicted of arbitrariness and unreasonableness. This is, to be sure, an over-simplification of the matter. Before either giving in to a demonstration or throwing it out, one has the right to know the presuppositions upon which it rests, for one thing. But granted all such conditions, the above is the aim of philosophical argument. It is probably true that this aim always falls short of realization, but it remains the aim nonetheless.

The fact that few people in a given age are convinced by the philosophical proofs for something does not alter this intent of serious metaphysical argument. The theist, for instance, is committed to the task of proving God's existence, the non-theist to the task of disproving His existence. In our times the proofs of the theist, at least (although some people are generous enough to include the proofs of the non-theist—is this true of the humanists?), are widely judged to be "unconvincing." It may well be that the age doesn't have it in for God particularly. Perhaps the age suspects any rational ground for believing in anything, and it may have been encouraged so to distrust reason by the fantastic preachment that a *reason* is always a *rationalization* (a neat example of a self-contradictory theory, incidentally).

But now the question is, why are the proofs for God's existence pronounced unconvincing? It is absurd simply to assume that the proofs are all defective, in one way or another, and that this sad fact has finally gotten all the way home even to the "popular mind." And it is also absurd to claim that some philosopher or other—generally Kant—has disposed once and for all of such proofs and so since Kant no one takes seriously the task

of proving God's existence. Opinion samplers may be permitted
to talk this way, but philosophers have no excuse for it. As philosophers they are rather concerned with the revision of arguments that have been shown to be defective, or with the revision
of criticism of arguments, where the criticisms have been shown
to be inadequate and misconceived. Therefore we see again that
the aim of philosophical argument is to compel rationally the
assent of the mind, even though some minds will persist in lean-
ing more heavily upon non-rational grounds for belief—such as
what all right-thinking people are thinking at any given time—
than upon rational grounds.

This is but to say that the aim of philosophical inquiry and
argument is *certainty*. Certainty is the state of being *rationally*
satisfied with an interpretation of experience. It does not pre-
clude the possibility of error, for throughout we are dealing with
such certainty as a finite mind can enjoy. There is no precise
rule determining when the mind has the right to be satisfied,
although certain negative rules can be cited, e.g., that one ought
to be uneasy in the presence of paradox and self-contradiction.
Because of this lack of theoretical precision it is tempting to set
aside the ideal of certainty and take up with the ideal of probability. This is a very great mistake, however unavoidable it may
seem in an age in which the widely-heralded "probabilism" of
scientific method has made so many notable advances. It is a
mistake because it merely assumes that metaphysical philosophy
has precisely the same aim as science and for that reason must
adopt the same methods. This is not the case, except in the pursuit
of the very general aim of knowledge and truth—an aim so general that it does not in itself determine the method proper to
each. Moreover, "probabilism" in metaphysics is meaningless
save on the presupposition of certainty in the sense just defined
above. He who says, "probability is the guide of life" and who
wants his viewpoint to be taken seriously must have adequate
reasons for believing this. These reasons should be all that a

reasonable man could ask. He is not able to demonstrate the truth of his belief "geometrically," but he supposes that the mind can rest in this belief, that, in other words, it has attained certainty. Otherwise he would have to say, "probability is probably the guide to life, the chances are this is the case." But again, the judgment that probability is probably, or possibly, the guide must rest on adequate grounds, if it is to be rationally compelling. Anybody, upon fair inspection of those grounds, ought to be able to see that probability is *really* the guide. A reasonably intelligent and fair-minded person, in other words, should be able to see that this judgment rests upon a *certain* apprehension of the nature of the world—not its whole nature, to be sure, but upon a real and significant aspect of the world.

The same must be said of the "trial and error" method, which is actually, I suppose, a kind of loose re-statement of "probabilism." This method is philosophically meaningful only upon the supposition of certainty, not certainty about every specific feature of the world as it is revealed in and to experience, but certainty at the really critical points. Unless "trial and error" were successful in disclosing a significant pattern in the world, about which we could be certain, it could not be a way of *knowing* at all. Actually there are many such significant patterns exhibited in experience (the atom is one, the electro-magnetic field is one, mathematics and aesthetics abound in them, morality discloses still others, etc.), and metaphysics is the immense and inescapable task of relating these patterns to one another within an inclusive pattern.

It is meaningless to say of such an inclusive pattern that it is probably true, unless one means that it *may* be true, that the pieces *can* be put together that way. But *must* they be so together? Every metaphysician of any real consequence in the history of western culture has believed that the system he provided had that imperative character. This seems arrogant, but it would be childish on our part to dismiss the claim simply on that account, for we cannot ask sensibly of a metaphysical system that it be modest and humble, that it substitute maidenly blushes and stammering for bold assertion and unresting pursuit of cogent and compelling argument. What we can call for are just such arguments; and where they are not forthcoming, we are right in looking upon that system as something that *might* be believed in as a poetic vision, as something that may or may not be entertained by the reader of that poetry, as his feelings and as his general awareness of life and the world seem to allow or to command.

The theist accepts the aim or ideal of certainty. Theism is not something that *might* be true, that might be believed as an interesting option among others. It is true, and its truth must be shown forth. How has theism gone about this?

First of all it is of capital importance to prove that God exists, the kind of God roughly described in Chapter II. Such proof, if successful, could hardly be expected to make a person religious, and it would very likely take a great deal more than that to make him Christian, but as a minimum it would clarify his understanding of God.[4]

In the presentation of the theistic proofs I shall not resort to the formal patterns traditionally employed. I shall try rather to state the essential contention of each of the proofs, and the kind of analysis of experience upon which it rests.

I. The A Posteriori Arguments

These arguments are based upon some feature of the commonly experienced world. They all attempt to prove that God or

---

[4] Some Christian theologians seem to feel that such proofs reveal an irreligious and unchristian streak in man's mind. They say that the human reason cannot hope to reach God, to "master" God. This contention is fatally ambiguous. To prove God's existence is not to master Him or even to aspire to master Him, any more than proofs for the existence of the external world have as their intent to reduce that world to a plastic passive instrument. Quite the contrary in fact in both instances: the intent of the proofs is to show that the mind has hold of something, and is held by something, other than mere ideas, in its knowledge of and dealings with the world and God.

infinite being is the only adequate and rationally satisfying explanation of that particular feature of the world and of the world as a whole. The nerve of these arguments is as follows:

Something exists, and it is finite.

The finite is not the cause of itself.

Neither can the finite in its whole or essential being be the effect of another finite entity.

Therefore the proper cause of this something is infinite, and this infinite being necessarily exists, and is God.

The root conviction here appears to be that finitude (limitation, dependency, etc.) presupposes infinitude as the source of its limitation and the support of its dependency. This is not a matter of mere definition or word-games. Everything experienced is finite; and nature, the system of finite entities, is itself finite, so far as we can reasonably judge, because there is no reason for supposing that the extension of nature indefinitely either forwards or backwards in time and in complexity lifts it beyond finitude. Indeed, one traditional approach in theism advocates for all it is worth the "infinitizing" of the finite, with the resultant breakdown either into mysticism or the denial of finitude altogether. Into mysticism: extend the series of finite causes far enough into complexity, the non-theist says, and *somehow* the series is able to produce itself out of itself. But *this* nature is ineffable and is incomprehensible. Into the denial of finitude: everything that exists is an aspect of infinite nature; indeed, any particular (and apparently finite) thing *is* infinite nature from a particular point of view. But this is impossible, for "the particular point of view" is just the problem; *limitation* of being, stubborn particularity and individuality are just what need to be accounted for.

There are many variations upon this theme in theism, but the theme is constant. Its important elements are: (1) Finitude and its application to all nature. Finitude characterizes everything in experience and experience itself. And then the claim is that a finite universe existing by itself is unthinkable—it would be an effect without adequate or sufficient cause. (2) The "causal law" or the principle of sufficient reason. Every event and every entity, and every configuration of events and of entities require a sufficient or adequate explanation and agency. The theist repudiates the idea of causation as mere uniformity of sequence; at this point he sides with common sense against tendencies in contemporary scientific thought. Cause is real agency, power that does things. This real agency is known both in the external world and in ourselves; and it is at the very least naïve to assume that this massive empirical knowledge was somehow put out of court entirely by the philosopher Hume, who, with the rest of us, was *compelled* to believe in real agency every time he raised his arm to scratch his neck (he denies of course that the compulsion is rational). (3) The necessity of the infinite as the unlimited and the inclusive. It has frequently been argued that the finite does not require the infinite as its cause, but only a (perhaps immeasurably) greater finite, perhaps a greater finite in the form of the cooperation of an indefinitely large number of other finites. The theistic rejoinder to that is that such proposals spring from an inadequate analysis of "finite." The cooperation of finites with one another does not lift them beyond finitude, for the fact of their cooperation itself requires explanation, and this explanation cannot be any one of the factors or entities taken up into this system. The cause of the system of finites is itself infinite, self-subsistent being. This infinite being, again, is not nature or the universe but the God who is the transcendent cause of nature and the universe. It is not nature because "nature" is either a name for the sum total of all finite substances and their modes of activity and their inter-relationships, in which case nature is not itself an individual and could not properly be said to be the cause of anything; or nature is an all-inclusive, infinite substance and individual, in which case the finite is but a mode or aspect of the one individual and the original problem has been lost, viz., the cause of the finite. Cause and effect are no longer twain but one. And therefore the infinite being that necessarily exists is God and not nature or the universe.

The "necessity" of the infinite means also that this being alone of all beings cannot fail to exist. Everything other than God is the kind of being that can fail to exist; and the universe is the system of things that can and do come into existence and go out of existence. But throughout all this changing scene God remains self-identical, the eternal ground of all change and the transcendent cause of every changeful being.

These affirmations and arguments all express the conviction that the infinite is apprehended with the finite and that the finite could not be apprehended as such save on the condition of a prior apprehension of the infinite. In the proofs we have been considering—commonly called cosmological—the mind rises from the finite to the infinite, but this is possible only because of the prevenience of the infinite.

This conviction also appears in the Augustinian argument from the degrees of being and value. According to that argument we should not be able to make judgments of relative value and of degrees of being unless the standard for such judgments were known to us. This standard is absolute perfection, or God.

This "cosmological" conviction is the core of another line of argument. Finite being is limited being. But this limitation requires explanation, because there is no reason apparent in the finite itself why it should be *this* being rather than *that,* why this kind of world rather than another, why one pattern of relationships rather than another; and we cannot rest in the answer, "Well, that is just the way it is." *Why* should it be that way?— this question ought not to be evaded. The theistic reply to that question is that limitation either argues purpose or it is ultimately inexplicable. Now the retreat into ultimate inexplicabilities is hazardous indeed, because it can easily turn into a rout—it can lead to an obscurantist mentality, an incorrigible, lazy-minded agnosticism. And therefore back of mystery or beyond it we must, as rational creatures, seek at least the vague looming shadow of intelligibility and rationality. Thus, back of limitation, of finitude, we see purpose. This purpose is the purpose of an unlimited, all-inclusive being who of necessity is prior to the limited, exclusive and dependent. No rational *why* can be asked of the existence of such a being, for his being and will affirm all positive possibilities, exclude nothing of value.

At this point we are close to the strain of theistic argument that is known as "teleological." Theism as a whole is teleological metaphysics, through and through; and it is therefore not very much of a curiosity that specific proofs of teleological character should have been formulated in this tradition. The objective of this type of argument is to show that the many instances and levels of adaptations in the world are so many indications of a cosmic intelligence, which, by reason of its power and wisdom, may rightly be addressed as God. And behind all the permutations in the formal structure of this proof there is a persistent theme: though there may be chance *in* the universe, the universe itself is not the creature of chance but of intelligent purpose. The total environment in which our life is set is not a fortuitously functioning mechanism or organism. It is everywhere instinct with purpose. The theist contends that it cannot be intelligibly argued that mind and purposive behavior as we know it in ourselves and as we see it suggested, at least, elsewhere, have accidentally and fortuitously developed in a non-purposive environment, for a "non-purposive environment" necessarily means a non-mental, non-spiritual environment. (No real meaning can be given to the notion of a mind without purpose; and no real meaning can be given to purpose without mind or spirit.) Such an "unplanned for" development would mean that mental processes, such as reasoning and willing, have been caused or produced by non-mental processes and are still being so caused. But it is clearly impossible to argue (i.e., to *reason*) for such a position with any consistent conviction that the argument itself is a significant factor in the determination of a mind; and therefore it remains an opinion bereft of all rational grounds. It will not do, then, to suppose that purposeful activity is limited to the human enterprise and that all else in nature, so far as we can read her, is blind and mindless action.[5] For our minds, our intelligent purposing, have not made the world in which we live, nor have they created our own fundamental natures. They are not responsible for (although they are responsible *to*) the basic scheme. And it will not do to suppose that "man is organic with nature" and then hasten to strike out of nature what is so truly human, that is, purpose-controlled activity, leaving man "the witty, canny child of a witless mother." Over against such notions theism stands for the acknowledgement of the genuine kinship of man and nature as participants in the cosmic order and plan of God.

Finitude is a pervasive characteristic of the world. Purposeful adaptation and arrangement is another such characteristic. We are now turning a line of argument that is concerned with the interpretation of a uniquely human realm, that of morality, the recognition and pursuit of moral values. This line of argument was first explicitly formulated by Kant, who, after destroying, to his own satisfaction, the rational certainty of theistic (and all other) metaphysics, turned to reasonable belief in most of the cardinal tenets of theism, predicated upon the bed-rock practical certainties of moral experience. The central motif of this sort of argument is that moral experience reveals data that metaphysics

---

[5] This supposition is of course made both by knowledgeable and subtle naturalistic metaphysicians and by persons more prone to psychologizing significant theories away than to meeting them on their own grounds. The latter are acutely conscious of the danger that in believing the world purposeful man may be deceived and deluded by his wishes. Well, so he might. But if man is lured by his desire into asking too much of the world, he is also tricked by fear into asking too little. Moreover, one may be cozened by his desire into believing something true as well as something false. I may be passionately eager to believe in the loyalty of a friend, but my passionate desire is surely no good ground for spitting at him as a traitor the next time I see him.

must acknowledge, such as the sense of unqualified obligation. Only if a God exists as the shaper and governor of the moral environment which in turn shapes and molds us, do such data make any real sense. Again, the argument is put in these terms: morality discloses a world deeper and richer than the natural, space-time world, in which richer world we feel called upon to make an unqualified response to the right and the good, even though the "natural man's" happiness and life may be forfeited thereby. A good man does his duty, though the heavens fall in upon him. But the good is not really good if the world systematically penalizes and frustrates its pursuit. Therefore, again, the world in which this seems to happen is not the ultimately real world. *That* world is one in which moral worth is honored all the way through; it is a supremely rational world and one therefore at all essential points under the control of a supreme mind.

There are some theists who do not accept this argument as cogent or compelling, but theists agree in general that concern for the good is not merely a human concern. The creation and enjoyment of value is the main business of the universe and of God.

Over against this stands the position of the humanist, for whom the creation and enjoyment of value is strictly a human concern, although nature produces man, the value-creator, and sustains him throughout all his activities. But only in the case of man do we have end-controlled activity. All other activity is devoid of rhyme and reason. To provide a negative support for this position the humanist occasionally, if not habitually, attributes perplexing sentiments to the theist. Theism, he says, claims that the values man enjoys really would not be values if God, the supreme good, did not exist; and, God alone is or has real value and everything else is value-less. Now it may be that Christian theologians and poets may now and then have spoken so injudiciously as that; but it is not the characteristic state of mind of Christian thinkers; and as far as I know, no theistic metaphysician of any consequence has ever believed these things that the humanist imputes to him. There is no reason why the theist cannot say with anybody else that values are really there to be appreciated, to be realized, and to be understood in relation to the total scheme of things. Theism stresses particularly, and quite clearly far more than humanism does, this last point: that of trying to understand how human concerns and achievements fit into the total environment. Or again, there is no reason for denying that values are what they are even if their status outside of human appreciation is either doubtful or non-existent. Even if we knew that the entire race were doomed shortly to disappear into everlasting night, while it is yet day we should admire veracity, courage and loyalty. We could not really do otherwise, for the larger part, though some might spend the last hours reviling their fate and cursing God, or in a last wild orgy try to blunt the spirit's torment. But all would put in the time in such pursuits as seemed good under the circumstances.

It is the task of the philosopher to evaluate these pursuits of truth and of value and the judgments and perceptions from which they arise. His aim is not to call in question, upon first acquaintance, the good that men seek. His aim is rather, as a metaphysician, to see what kind of sense the picture makes as a whole. And the theistic metaphysician believes that the clearest and best sense appears when human values, and our whole life and the life of all nature, are seen as expressions of a divine will and purpose, when all that is creaturely and finite is seen over against the eternal and the infinite.

II. The A Priori Argument

So far arguments based upon some experienced feature of the world or upon some all-pervasive characteristic of the world, have been reviewed. A very different kind of proof proceeds directly from the inspection of the definition of the idea of God to the rationally inescapable conclusion that such a being really exists. This argument, known as "ontological," was first explicitly formulated by Anselm (1033-1109). It has been viewed with suspicion by many theists, and in its primitive form it is now supported by no one. It has also been frequently revived and revised after apparently annihilating criticism. In its primitive form the argument is based upon the standard definition of God as that being than which none greater can be conceived. If such a being were only an idea, only a possibility, then indeed a greater being *could* be conceived, namely one that actually or concretely existed. But by definition no being can be greater than God, and therefore God necessarily exists, not merely as or in idea, but really.

The intent of the argument is to show that non-existence cannot be seriously and intelligently predicated of God, that is, the attempt to do so results in self-contradiction. If this is so, then the mind, so far as it thinks God at all, must think of him as actually existing, notwithstanding verbal denials of his existence. Against this claim it has frequently been argued that the entire argument is deposited at the outset in the definition of God. This is of course the case, and the adherents of the argument have rarely considered it a damaging criticism, since the purpose of any formal deductive argument is to show what is contained in the prime definitions of the argument. So here: the argument intends to show what one lets himself in for when he uses the term "God" seriously. The being to whom this term properly applies *cannot* be a mere possibility; He alone among all beings *must* exist.

In spite of its failure to win a large following of admirers this argument has a remarkably perennial character, largely, I think, because of its profoundly religious character rather than because of any logical power or neatness and simplicity. The religious sentiment embedded in it concerns the all-sufficiency of God, God's perfect power of being. The argument really derives, then from the conviction that God is the "cause," the whole explanation, of His own nature and existence, and therefore no appeal is made to the nature of the experienced world, but only to the idea of God and what it contains. It might then be said with substantial justification that this proof above all the others discloses the intent of proof that deals with the ultimate problems of human life, because it sets forth what is already apprehended in the idea of God, quite as though the only way one could possibly prove the existence of God would be by beginning with God, for if one began anywhere else, could he ever really reach from that which is not God to God Himself?

III. The Appeal to Religious Experience

In recent times, largely because of the influence of Kant's criticism of the more traditional arguments, arguments for God based upon religious experience have appeared in theistic thought. The fundamental claims of such arguments are that there are irreducibly *religious* data that must be accounted for by any philosophy aiming at comprehensiveness and that the reality of God, the religious object, is the only adequate way of accounting for these data. The data identified as irreducibly religious are the deeply-ingrained impulsion to worship (something in the world elicits from man a worshipful response, arouses the sense of awe and reverence), the mystical awareness of God, and the practical results of the religious life. These data can be adequately understood only if they are seen to be the effect in the human spirit of relation to religious reality, or God.

This argument is a fairly close relative of the argument *consensus gentium* and of the pragmatic argument. "The plain man" is wont to say that where there's a lot of smoke there must be at least a little fire. So the almost universal presence of religious concern in mankind argues at least a dim awareness of a religious environing reality. And again, whether or not the religious life hooks into anything *out there,* it can be made to produce something good *in here;* and until definite and unmistakable word is forthcoming from *out there,* the good fruit of practical religious living may be said to be the truth of religious belief.

Odd as it may seem, neither of these arguments cuts much of a figure in traditional theism, and in revisionary theism they are frequently given a cool reception also. (In those circles neither of these contentions is regarded as philosophical argument, however suggestive they may be for religion as a whole.) In fact, the humanists seem more impressed with both of them than at least the traditional theists are. The humanist is not prepared to abandon religion; he wants to put it right and keep it going. Accordingly religion is rightly regarded as a universal phenomenon, for it shows man everywhere concerned with making the most of himself. And the fruit of religion, the good fruit that is, is the measure of its truth: a good religion is one that assists man in the integration of himself; a false religion is one that impedes and confuses this integration.

The theistic conception of God will not permit so insular a view of religion and of the religious quest as this. If God exists, it is entirely possible and perhaps inevitable that all men should have a dim and confused awareness of Him, and that here and there this dim awareness of Him should be clarified and sharpened into a dazzling focus (mysticism). If God exists, then the prime concern of religious activity and ultimately of all our activity is to bring us into the most positive and productive relationships with Him in whom is fullness of life. If God exists, then the "data" of religious experience are in the main veridical and reliable. And then the arguments from religious experience may test the data by the theistic affirmation and weigh the theistic affirmation by the light of religious experience.

. . . If God exists. If he does not exist, then the view of religion as a useful instrument for the achievement of integration may sweep the horizon with our indifferent blessing or with our curse, as we each privately see fit. But better yet, in that case, to part soberly with the trappings and symbols of religion, for if there is no properly adorable deity, then to avoid madness for as long as we can we must refuse every temptation to worship anything else, whether it be the ideal potentialities of mankind or the stupidly fecund womb of nature.

In the end everything in the Christian faith turns upon the existence of God, and therefore everything rides upon the metaphysic of theism. We shall now see that this does not mean that the whole content of that faith can be gotten out of theism. It cannot. Yet without that metaphysic, without that "abstract" approach to deity, without that attempt to make the theory of divine existence rationally compelling, the riches and grandeur of that faith could be written down as ambitious poetry, or perhaps as a noble ethic resting upon arrant superstition.

IV. Theism and the Christian Faith

THE CHRISTIAN FAITH is much wider and deeper than a metaphysical system. Much of its unique teaching is set forth as revealed truth, as wisdom beyond the reach of the unassisted human reason, as wisdom and knowledge divinely communicated and divinely guaranteed. The problem now is to see how, in Christianity, the metaphysic of theism is related to this higher and wider knowledge. In this connection only the doctrines of sin and salvation, and of immortality, will be dealt with, partly because of limitations of space and partly because these doctrines have an absorbing interest for many humanists.

There is no strictly theistic view of sin or of salvation.[1] This is because both terms designate conditions and activities not open to normal inspection and judgment. Both deal with the "hidden life of the soul" in relation to God, although both have outward manifestations. This means that a man is not a sinner because he is immoral, i.e., he is a glutton, an adulterer, a miser etc.; but he is immoral because he is a sinner. His outer life, his life in the world and among his fellows is wrong because the roots of his being have suffered a violent wrenching, and he has no power in himself to cure this radical trouble. If he is to be made whole at all, God alone must do it. And so man is not saved because he is virtuous and filled with all the beauteous fruits of the spirit. He is

---

[1] Calvin's ideas on these doctrines are surely predicated upon the supposition that God exists, but Calvin would as surely be among the last to claim that even the most enlightened human mind could penetrate the mysteries of sin and salvation. According to Calvin, the Christian believes in these because the Bible, the Word of God, teaches them. And thus again we must note how unfortunate it is to take Calvin as the chief spokesman for theistic metaphysics.

filled with all these fruits because what was terribly distorted in the "depths" of his being has been put right by God Himself, who alone adequately knows the secret places of the spirit and who alone can forgive sin, that is, who alone can restore the spirit to productive relationships to the perfect good and the full life.

The Christian faith teaches that to know oneself as sinner, and not simply as wrong-doer, and to know the promise of salvation, and not merely to experience happiness or to feel virtuous, are possible only if one knows more of God than reason (and therefore metaphysics) comprehends. Theism holds that God has created man in and for freedom and that the plan of relationships between God and man is personal and ethical, not mechanical and neutral. But theism has no way of telling how much of Himself God puts into that plan, or whether in certain events God "lays bare His soul" and "comes nigh unto His children." Theism may speak of divine love as concern but it does not comprehend divine grace "laying its glory by" and dwelling among men "full of grace and truth." And theism knows nothing of sin as the rejection of grace or of salvation as the Hound of Heaven—of grace that persists in the face of rejection.

Yet theism has something to say about this wisdom and knowledge beyond the reach of our rational powers. For one thing these more full-bodied teachings of the faith must be prevented from toppling over the edge of intelligibility into rank absurdity. Even if they are "beyond reason," they are formulated at least by human minds and are addressed to human minds, and this means that there can be no holiday for the spirit of honest and relentless criticism in the utterance and organization of the purest and profoundest insights of faith. The deeply pious Christian may celebrate the greatness and goodness of God by describing himself as nothing or worse than nothing; but the tender protestations of this piety are not to be taken literally, because the person here is not talking metaphysics, he is using the language of devotion, of poetic, religious communication. God could not create a *nothing,* a literal non-entity. And so long as this "nobody" can praise the Almighty he is something rather than nothing. But the utterance of piety cannot literally mean either that in the sight of God the person has no value, is a worthless, miserable wretch. Whatever God has created has value, and the worthlessness which the sinner hymns and confesses is not determined by his measuring himself against the perfection of God, but it is determined by his measuring himself against what he himself ought to be. If theism is true, there can be no direct comparison of the worth of the finite with the perfection of God. It may be possible to compare the worth of one creature with the worth of another ("are ye not of much more value than they?"), but between created being and uncreated being there can be no direct comparison. Thus no creature is rightly regarded as a poor thing simply because it is not God. Indeed, man alone is a disgraced and disgraceful creature because he renounces his distinctive station, now aspiring to the level of deity and now trying to turn and live as the animals. But man's disgrace is *not* that he falls short of deity.

The erection of barriers against absurdities is not the only contribution of metaphysical philosophy to the right apprehension of the Christian faith. It can also rightly aspire to throw some positive light upon the mysteries. For example, the faith affirms certain things about the eternal order and the temporal order. Among these we find not only the belief that God Himself is timeless being but also that the eternal "erupts" into the temporal order, specifically in the incarnation of Christ. Now if God is timeless being and is also living spirit, the finite mind has a great puzzle before it. The metaphysician may err in claiming that he can either solve that puzzle or rule it out of bounds, but he is right in attempting to throw as much light upon it as possible. If, then, for whatever reasons (for the purpose of the argument let us suppose them valid) Christian theology teaches the timelessness of God, it must not also teach the *pre-determination* of temporal events by the divine will, except by way of concession to the earth-bound mind of man, because for God there can be no "before and after" in our sense. His will cannot strictly be the *antecedent* cause of an effect in time. Accordingly Christian thought must acknowledge that God's determination of events and entities is essentially different from any mode of causal agency visible to us. God's causal agency must be "contemporaneous" with the event itself. Thus a subtle metaphysician like Augustine speculates that the divine experience is an eternal "now," an all-inclusive present "moment" of awareness or perception in which the full span of time, of temporal successiveness, is comprehended. God is aware of such temporal successiveness, but *His* experience, unlike ours, is not defined by such successiveness. Whether or not such a notion is really intelligible or deeply suggestive if intelligible, it illustrates how the metaphysical enterprise in Christian thought trenches upon the ultimate mysteries.[2]

It is another question whether a central Christian doctrine is compatible with theistic principles. Consider in this conection the doctrine of the incarnation. The incarnation may not be inconsistent with theism although theism does not imply the incarnation. In traditional thought the incarnation is an "event," a concrete historical event: the birth, life, ministry, crucifixion and resurrection of Jesus Christ. The occurrence of one event rather than another cannot be "deduced" from a metaphysical principle, and therefore only in a very loose sense can it be said that a the-

---

[2] Calvin's attitude towards metaphysical speculation even in the service of the faith is strikingly similar to that revealed occasionally by the humanists. Calvin believed that speculation should not range far, if at all, beyond the biblical text and the Old Catholic interpretations of same. On the whole he seems to have had an incurable suspicion of any metaphysical curiosity. The humanists for their part wish to stick close to the text of scientific method and look askance at the far-ranging problems of metaphysical philosophy. Professor Auer's description of humanism as "puritanism with a sense of humor" is not then so far afield as it looks—even though one hears but seldom of a humanist who died laughing at the plight of contemporary man.

istic principle covers or applies to this event or series of events, namely, the principle of divine love or concern. But that principle does not determine nor anticipate in what concrete ways that divine love will express and reveal itself. Again, that principle may help in the understanding or interpretation of the incarnation, and surely Christian theologians have drawn freely upon metaphysics in the interpretation of the incarnation, but no principle in the metaphysics of theism *demands* such an event. Therefore if a Christian believes in the incarnation it is not because it is "theistic" but because he believes "this is the way it was." His appeal is to history and to the "permanent revolution" of history that he believes he grasps in Jesus Christ.

This is the case also with the particular schemes of providence which Christian theologians have devised to interpret the scriptural witness. No one of them is a strict deduction from the fundamental tenets of theism. Theism is bound to say that God's wisdom and power direct the world and human history to their respective fulfillment. Theism is bound to say that such direction cannot be at any point a violation of the freedom of finite spiritual agents. But theism is *not* bound to say that such-and-such specific occurrences (for instance, the unexpected reversal of the direction of an infection) are the effects of the immediate and redemptive presence of God, because the theist can get no farther than the general description of the general pattern of the divine being and the divine activity. That God is against evil, this he may say. He may be expected to submit an opinion on why God permits evil and on the "natural history" of evil and on whether God feels compassion for the victims of evil in a way analogous to our compassion. But as to whether God is uniquely present in or to certain events and certain persons for the fulfillment of His comprehensive aims, this metaphysics cannot decide.

There is no standard opinion in the theistic perspective on the question of why evil is tolerated by God. ("Tolerated" is wrong of course, since it is a uniform theistic conviction that God is always acting to overcome evil, and therefore he does not merely "tolerate" it.) Some say it is because He knows the world is ultimately richer for it, that is, evil exists in order to be overcome, and the righteous power released to overcome it creates more good than would otherwise have been realized.[3] Other theists contend that evil is embedded in the ultimate nature of things (at least in the form of suffering and pain, though probably not in the form of wickedness) and God himself has to acknowledge its radical character and struggle against it.[4] But all agree that the worst of these evils, in the color and range of its effects, is moral evil; and all are agreed in tracing this to the incredibly hazardous gift of freedom; and all are agreed that God voluntarily accepts the hazards, and that all who cherish freedom also cheerfully accept the hazards that freedom entails.

One conspicuous element of what generally passes for theism has so far been overlooked. That is immortality. In the "average" religious mind as we encounter it in our culture God and immortality are indissolubly wedded. Can this bond stand the test of objective scrutiny?

It is sometimes held that a theistic conception of God is compatible with the denial of personal immortality[5] and that most of the Old Testament is ample evidence for this. The latter part of the assertion, at least, is in error. The conception of God that prevails in much Old Testament religion is only partly theistic, because the essential note of man as created in-and-for-freedom, of man as a participant in the freedom of God, is lacking there.

---

[3] As formulated here this position is closer to that of Josiah Royce (cf. *The Problem of Christianity*) than to traditional theistic theodicy; but I believe that there is much in the traditional views that suggests this interpretation.

[4] This view is held by Edgar Brightman (cf., among other works, his *Philosophy of Religion*) and probably also by Charles Hartshorne.

[5] This is the only kind of immortality discussed here. "Social" immortality, the "survival" of the individual in the memory of other individuals and in the values he helped to create, is of course no immortality at all, metaphysically considered.

This does not mean that "unfreedom" is specifically taught (although it is implied here and there). It does mean that freedom is not specifically affirmed. Furthermore, while the theistic note of divine purposeful activity is present virtually from the beginning, it is only late in the development of Old Testament religion that the Hebrew rises to the apprehension of love as defining the ultimate pattern of relations between God and man. When finally this love is apprehended, Judaism is well on its way toward the affirmation of individual immortal blessedness in communion with God.[6]

The theist is committed to the belief that, however persons may ultimately be disposed of, this cannot be in a way that violates personal existence or the fundamental conditions of selfhood. *This violation would cheat the divine plan or aim of its fulfillment, which is impossible.* Would death itself be such a violation? There is no self-evident answer to this question. The answer depends on whether we regard death as the collapse of physiological processes *without which spirit cannot continue.* If this is death, then spirit seems to be at the mercy of non-personal forces after all. Could this be the divine intent, that spirit should finally bow before the stress of flesh? To most theists, and to some who are not theists, this is not the case. The spirit was created for a richer destiny than that and so it persists beyond death in the pursuit and in the enjoyment of that destiny.

Here the theistic position is that God creates persons not as instrumentalities to be brushed away when their usefulness is

---

[6] In the most primitive Hebrew traditions God had not the power to award everlasting blessedness. His sovereignty did not reach into Sheol (Hell) and therefore the souls of the departed were beyond His control. When at last the power was imputed to Him, He had not the concern or infinite solicitude for the person as such but only for the nation or folk. It is astonishing and deeply moving to read Hosea's poignant celebration of the divine solicitude for the people: here is God pouring out His deepest personal concern for an impersonal unity, the people. The time was not yet at hand for this contradiction to be thrown off and for One to preach and Himself to show forth the divine solicitude reaching out redemptively even to the lowliest human derelict.

past but as ends-in-themselves.[7] They may not be the only such
ends, and a universe is conceivable without them, but granted
their existence, that is what they are. Neither is it necessary to
suppose the rest of nature to have been created simply for the
sustenance and enjoyment of such remarkable creatures (although there is certainly a tendency in theism to believe that the
purpose of God can be more clearly read in the higher creatures).
Nevertheless theism contends that spirit is not victimized in the
end by the rest of nature. Therefore if a man dies, that is, is anni-
hilated, it is *not* because physiological processes in the end call
the tune; it is ultimately because he is worth no more to the Lord
of the Universe, he has no potentialities worth preservation and
enhancement. *This a theist cannot consistently believe.* And here
a kind of negative argument for immortality comes to the surface: *no sufficient reason can be given for the extinction of spirit.*

Traditionally theists have bolstered the case by appeal to the
evidence. It is not quite the case that all theists have been unqualified mind-matter dualists (certainly the Thomists are not, and the
idealistic theists are not); yet most of them accept the common-
sense conviction that mind and body are distinguishable and that
mind enjoys a significant measure of independence and freedom
in relation to the body. For example, in *reasoning,* in any case of
systematic reflection upon something, we know a unique kind of
activity which in all likelihood is accompanied by a very complex
pattern of physiological activity. Now it seems possible to say that
reasoning is just one way the brain behaves, but this notion has no
more than a superficial plausibilty at best. Reasoning is not the
way the *brain* behaves; it is the way a *mind* operates. Epistemo-
logically the brain is the name for a constellation of perceived
qualities to which, in relation to the entire physico-chemical uni-

---

[7] Unfortunately Christian theology has not always held consistently to this
view. Consider a classical conception of why God saves any men at all when
all so richly deserve eternal damnation: God wants a few to bring the regiments
of the heavenly hosts up to the perfect number which was broken by the fall of the
wicked angels. This is going a long way around in the interests of tidiness.

verse certain "powers" or activities are imputed. The brain does nothing as an agent, in the proper sense, so far as the immediate testimony of experience runs: it acts or reacts in accordance with the patterned flux of energy, or is simply a part of that patterned flux. Yet "with the brain" the mind *thinks;* it perceives the world, it imagines hypotheses, it deduces conclusions, it wills activities of the whole self. This must mean either that the mind calls for the kind of brain-activity necessary for such unique and specific mental processes, or, that these mental processes can use equally well a variety of brain-states or neural patterns. It seems very difficult if not impossible to really discover which of these is the case; but I find it very hard to believe that one configuration of neural activity is called for by an erroneous or mistaken line of reasoning, e.g., a fallacious syllogism, and another configuration for a correct line of reasoning; or, again, that one "brain-phase" goes along with the idea "God" and another with the thought of the Devil (although all sorts of psychosomatic signs doubtless appear in conection with each, such as rapid pulse, flushed cheeks, sulphurous taste in the mouth etc. when "Devil" is thought). But if this *is* the case, then the *mind* does the selecting of the proper neural patterns, or at any rate it *can* do so.

The common-sense judgment is that the *person* makes up his own mind, really wills, really thinks. The theist agrees. He too believes that the body is partly susceptible of direction and control; and that this direction and control originates in the self itself. He too believes that when he thinks, this is not primarily the result of indiscernible activities in the universal system of physico-chemical energy; and that when he wills, this is not a bewitching illusion miraculously tossed up on the heaving sea of purpose-less energy.

We have just come through a rough illustration of the kind of interpretation of the mind-body problem that many theists follow in the discussion of immortality. Its objective is to show that even our limited minds can see that spirit is not the "thing," the product, of physiological processes but to the contrary can establish a partial mastery over such processes. And in this interpretation we also see again the major principle: the human spirit is not simply a "natural" product, a complex organism. It is unique being with unique value, unique aspirations, and unique facilities for the realization of these aspirations. These may all be called "natural" provided we mean "native or essential to man." To call them natural in any other sense tends either to blur what is irreducibly human into a wider and vaguer environment in which, accordingly, we lose sight of the genuinely unique in man; or unwittingly to invest that wider and vaguer environment with a human character and value we do not know it possesses; or both.

The belief in immortality in itself does not logically entail the belief that the human spirit is not really at home in this world and in the flesh. It is true that Christianity has sometimes come up with the kind of "otherworldliness" that humanists seem tempted to identify with theism as such. Let us not linger longer at the graveside of that poor creature, for it is no fairer a representative of theism or of Christian thought than the nihilistic pessimism of Sartre is of humanism. The attitude, so central to the humanistic position, of "this earth is enough" has frequently enough been captured by the extremists who mean by it: "Merrily [or lugubriously; take your pick; nothing comes back from the wash anyway] we go to hell"—an attitude deplored by the sober humanists who sing "Work for the night is coming" with dignity and with suitable emendations in the original text. So also the attitude, "This earth is not all" has frequently enough been taken over by the extremists who mean by it: "This earth stinks, and accursed be he whose nostrils are not offended by it"—an attitude deplored by theists and by Christians.

The theistic avowal of immortality is part and parcel of the whole perspective and particularly of the belief that the whole creation moves toward its fulfillment. This fulfillment includes the divine sustaining and the divine renewal of the human spirit through and beyond death, so that the will of man shall be perfected, which is to say that men may become the creators and enjoyers of the value which is written into the basic pattern of human life.

The Christian community may have additional information concerning the eternal life but the metaphysician has the right to claim that this information cannot contradict the little that is metaphysically ascertainable. And so again we conclude: the full content of Christian life and belief is much richer than the metaphysics of theism can possibly comprehend. Yet theism is woven into the whole fabric of that life and faith.

V. Theism and the Good

ONLY IN THE MOST GENERAL TERMS can it be said that there is a theistic ethical and social philosophy. This is simply to say that no one ethical system follows strictly from the fundamental principles of metaphysics. From the nature of God no set of moral injunctions can be directly derived, and from the theistic conception of man no specific system of moral values can be deduced. Nevertheless some interpretations of morality are much more consistent with theistic principles than certain other interpretations; and in general the Christian faith has presented a view of the good for man which is consonant with theism.

Again, to call this view "otherworldly" is to use a term that has richer emotional suggestion than descriptive power. Presumably use of the term expresses the judgment that Christianity and theism lure moral concern away from this life and its distressing problems in the direction of a mysterious and unattainable good "beyond the skies." Consequently when the eyes are riveted upon Beulah Land the feet are apt to wander into mire that could and should have been avoided. Moreover, the humanist says, "Theism and Christianity lead men to believe that nothing can be done about their oppressively wrong situations until and unless God deigns to assist and to redeem them." Such a preachment, the indictment continues, encourages civic irresponsibility and complacent acceptance of the *status quo*. Finally theism holds before man certain absolute values and declares him lost if he fails to acknowledge and realize them.

Very little of this has anything to do with the fundamental

principles of theism. The theist cannot consistently minimize the values of this world because this world is organically related to a wider world, and its values and purposes mesh into a wider purpose and good. Theism affirms that this world has a value and our career in it a significance that are not ephemeral and are not simply a *human* judgment. The creation and enjoyment of value is truly a cosmic concern and not merely man's attempt to dignify and enhance his own existence.

In such affirmations it is very hard fairly to see anything that should sap the nerve of moral endeavor. To the contrary, it may be reasonably supposed that many persons have been steadied and strengthened in great moral crises, and sustained in the choice of the harder part by the reflection that the cause was not lost though they perished and though "the race of man entire" vanished and by this whirling planet was quite forgotten. And this is but to say that neither logically nor psychologically is there pretext for abdication of ethical responsibility in the theistic perspective.

For the moment let us pursue the psychological and practical rather than metaphysical and logical principles by asking what would serve better to give the spirit "elbow-room" and "breathing-space," what would better avail to give men time to laugh and to play, than to believe that "if we live we live unto the Lord and if we die we die unto the Lord, so that living or dying we are the Lord's"? On the other hand, to feel the full and inexorable burden of value-creating upon one's shoulders, to believe that but for oneself and that holy fraction of the race that shares one's deepess convictions, the "world" of justice, mercy, peace and fundamental decency might well be lost—this is not a belief calculated to provide refreshment and shade from the ardors of the day. Nobility and pathos might well grace the soul on such terms, but the blessed comic spirit whose zest and jubilance we set too little store by, does not thrive there.

"Breathing-space" is not everything, and the comic is not the whole, though life without them is grim and tasteless. Let us then ask how these rival views, the theistic and the humanistic, illuminate the darker side, the side of high and firm resolve, the side of sober pursuit of the good. Particularly, let us ask how these rivals fare when the "time is short." What does each promise to do for us then? Take the apocalyptic ravings of atomic-warfare Jeremiahs at their most vivid. Suppose that the odds are staggeringly long against intelligence, education, and good-will, and very, very short on violence, malice and ignorance, so that the whole earthly future of the race swings out over the abyss. What is there now to steady the fluttering moral pulse and to check the wild surge of hysterical hate and fear, not to "save the race from extinction" (for we have for the moment supposed that impossible), but to give each person courage to speak the last lines of his piece clearly, to be a man to the end and not simply to posture and play the part? And what is there to suggest and to reinforce the *importance* of this latter course, the importance of being *human* to the end? After us, no one here to treasure our heroism, no one upon whose course to cast the sweet influence of beneficient example. The importance of that course remains, nonetheless, to the end, for at the last we must not renounce our own nature and spirit, even though the flesh cowers and whimpers before the stinging sweat and sickness of fear.

But let us not get so far out from the metaphysical base of operations. For theism the end of last man is not different, either in metaphysical or ethical principle, from the death of everyman. The world as a whole is not impoverished for long by the collapse of a civilization, the death of a person, or the extinction of the race,[1] because the potentialities of rational spirit are inexhaust-

---

[1] The humanist's position is very interesting at this point. He too is obliged to say that the obliteration of the race does not impoverish the cosmos, since all value-judgments are human and when humanity disappears all value-judgments and values will disappear. But the disappearance of value will not impoverish the cosmos, and this is surely the only possible case—if indeed *it* is possible—where loss of value does not mean impoverishment! On the other hand,

ible, and persons and societies of persons "dissolve" in one realm and are re-constituted afresh in another. And thus while tragedy is a unique dimension and ever-present reality of human experience, it does not set the frame-work or the boundaries of that experience, for tragedy is itself set in the framework of fulfillment and vindication of high aspiration and heroic sacrifice.

The purpose in individual personal existence must then be more than to enrich the society in which he lives or subsequent persons, as it must surely be more than to be "happy" in the conditions of this life. That purpose must be the fulfillment of the full range of potentialities resident in that spirit, since each is not merely an instrument of an other and since none is the plaything or pawn of God.

Does this commit the theist to a value-absolute, or perhaps to a system of absolute values? Does personality itself emerge as that supreme value, that end-in-itself? If this should turn out to be an inference from theistic principles, it is not what the humanist usually means when he claims that theism involves absolute moral values. He means that theism absolutizes a moral code, making it binding without qualification upon all men on the assumption that it is divinely legislated and not created by man himself. In the place of this arbitrary and inflexible ethic the humanist substitutes a relative and flexible system, recognizing

the humanist cannot claim that human existence enriches the cosmos, either. On his terms that would simply be our opinion, and with our disappearance there will be no opinion-holders. Accordingly, humanism believes that only man has value, but only value in and for himself. He is an island of value in a boundless sea of non-value. To the universe it is all one whether he lives or dies. Yet, he says, this man is an organic part of nature: and thus between value and non-value there is unbroken continuity. Between mere behavior and the good life, perfect continuity; between electrical charges and syllogisms and symphonies, perfect continuity; between visceral tensions and Calvary, perfect continuity. But does perfect continuity mean anything more than *underlying identity*? If not, then we must complain in season and out of season of the deceitfulness of the world, of language, of common-sense, and of every high-born sentiment within our hearts, that things at bottom one should by their senseless conspiracy be made to seem twain!

that virtue and vice have no stable particular meanings in the full sweep of human cultures. This substitution is proposed in the name of genuine reasonableness and for the sake of the ethical development of the human spirit. Obviously, the theist is obliged to give such a claim careful consideration.

What, then, does it mean to say that all moral values are relative? Professor Auer asserts that man, not God, is the measure of all things in respect to their value. This may mean: (1) It is man alone who makes value-judgments, and therefore it is man alone who knows if anything has or is value. Conceivably, if this were true, other things might have value apart from man. (1) is really quite an innocent notion, being but a special instance of the notion that man is the only creature *he* knows that is endowed with the power of cognition. An amoeba may have value, and may pursue value, but the amoeba doesn't *know* this (we suppose). It may be that we have slighted the amoeba here, but it is a risk we are probably entitled to take. (2) But "relativity of value" may also mean that other things have value only insofar as they are useful to man. Then man would not only be the only creature who knows values, he would be the only creature for whom values really are. (2) does not however decide the question whether *something* is unqualifiedly valuable or good. It simply asserts that whatever this might be it would have to be bound up and related to human life. And what then of human life? *Does it not automatically become an absolute, an underived and irreducible good?* For even if we were driven to concede that human life were derived from less developed creatures or even ultimately from a strange agitation in matter, the *value* of human life could not, on these terms, possibly be conceived of as *derivative,* since nothing has value save in relation to human life as we now experience it. Thus, if the humanist goes down this line (2) he is obliged at the end to confess either (a) absolutely nothing, including human life, *really* has value, or (b) human life, at least, is underivatively and unconditionally good.

Is (a) really a live option? No, it has a verbal sense only, because to deny value to everything compels one, again, either to say (i) the term "value" properly applies to absolutely nothing, or (ii) everything has *dis-value* (is evil). Neither (i) nor (ii) can be seriously entertained, because the possession of truth in any case is good, and neither of these alternatives can accommodate this fact. Therefore the humanist is left with the sole option: human life is unconditionally and underivatively good. This good is *not* relative to anything else.[2]

Another step must now be taken, because we have not yet moved into the realm of the sharper and more tragic moral problems. What, for instance, should be the rule when one must choose between his own life and the life of another? *Whose* life has absolute value? Whatever one chooses to do then, value will be lost, and, according to the humanist, will be irreparably lost. Should one act so as to confer more value upon the survivors or upon subsequent generations? But how shall we say *more* value? Is it humanity as a lump that has absolute value, or is it particular persons? If it is humanity as a whole, then individual life is simply instrumental to the perfection of the whole. And if a whole is this the present mass of mankind, or is it all men, past present and future? But why go farther? If I act in behalf of all men, I act for myself as well, since I am a man. If I act so that all men should be happy or should live in peace or should realize their potentialities, I am apparently acting so that *I* might enjoy these values also. *But if I am voluntarily sacrificing my life, I*

---

[2]Professor Auer has committed himself, it would seem, not only to the proposition that man is the absolute value, but also to the proposition that nothing else has any value. This view surely lacks "natural piety." Even though very few other creatures have cause to give thanks for the existence of man (there is no reason to believe that the plump cow of genetic experimentation is really any more *contented* than its primitive forbears), man should give thanks daily for the existence of those other creatures without which his own would be impossible. Moreover the humanist's view not only lacks natural piety—it is also further illustration of the invincible insularity of humanism, which, on the whole, is a kind of cosmological isolationism.

cannot seriously be hoping to enjoy these things myself. This act therefore involves my deliberately willing a privileged position for *others*. But this does not mean that he who so sacrifices himself considers himself a mere instrumentality. He affirms his own humanity, his own ethical individuality in his choice. The self-sacrifice is the fruit of his rational will and the affirmation of his own freedom.[3]

The question now arises, what metaphysical perspective affords the clearest and soundest justification for such action? The theistic answer is: that scheme in which the significance of rational will and of freedom is not made dependent upon non-human, mechanical, physico-chemical forces; that scheme in

---

[3] This freedom is always exercised within limits of varying tightness. The men of the submarine who chose to go down with the ship after it had been fatally hit had, after all, a fairly limited range of selection: certain (morally certain, not metaphysically certain) death if they stayed, almost certain death if they left (in fact only one survived). (The story is graphically told in *The Saturday Evening Post,* July 30, 1949, in an article entitled, "We Gave the Japs a Licking Underseas," by Vice-Admiral Charles A. Lockwood (ret.) and Percy Finch.

But man does not in the end really choose whether to live or to die, and that is one reason why his choices are never metaphysically certain. He may choose to expose himself to hazards that are ordinarily fatal. He may put a gun to his head and pull the trigger; but after he pulls the trigger the universe takes over, and the degree of penetration of his will into the cosmic pattern would seem to be relatively slight after he has willed the nullification of his will and of all such penetration *after* the act of nullifying his will. Paradoxically the suicide accordingly asserts his own will and surrenders himself absolutely to cosmic forces. He uses his freedom to destroy not merely his life but ideally to destroy his freedom and thus to become thing-like. The suicide does not will himself dead; he wills himself "unhuman," that is, beyond the endurance and the infliction of pain, beyond guilt, beyond responsibility, beyond harrowing novelty. To will annihilation is impossible: one can will only the existence of some of the conditions which ordinarily produce that effect. The suicide has always therefore to reckon with the possibility that the universe will toss him back into the problem alive from which he seeks escape through death. Now and then a suicide plots his own destruction with such cunning and protracted calculation that it could almost be said that he was plotting the murder of the universe rather than his own destruction. He means to destroy the resistance of the universe to his plans. And in fact the motive is there in many suicides—not of course quite to "murder the universe"—but to get at some one, to "kill" something in that person by the destruction of himself.

which the price paid for justice, peace, decency, is honored without qualification; that scheme in which sacrifice is both real and ultimately efficacious. If this scheme is in the main true, then men will do well to set freedom and honor, justice and love above happiness and life itself. If this scheme is false and its contradictory true, then men would do well to calculate more carefully the odds that favor survival above everything else—a course that the wisest men of all creeds have steadfastly rejected.

And now once more let it be asked whether from this view it can be legitimately inferred that men should abandon every stiff and sturdy effort to improve society and themselves? Does such a view of the world and of man and of God really serve for little ethically but to dull the smart of injustice? To make men content with inequitable and iniquitous social institutions? Professor Auer's affirmative answers to such questions are without remainder, so far as I can see, a function of the systematic and indefensible identification of theism with what he takes to be Calvinism. Now it is true that Calvinism glorifies the absolute sovereignty of God to the point where human freedom and power seem to evaporate, logically; but Calvinists, like all the rest of us, are saved from the logical implications of their own thought by the pressure of the work-a-day world and by the massive bulwark of "common-sense" wisdom. And therefore the Calvinists did not become quietists, who become morally flabby and irresponsible while they wait for the Lord. On Sunday the Calvinist merchant or sea-captain may have solemnly chanted: "Wait upon the Lord, O my soul"; but on Monday morning he didn't wait for anybody else.

The theistic avowal of ethical purpose regnant everywhere in the universe and of the transcendent power and goodness of God, does not entail the belief that "man can do nothing in his own behalf." If God exists, no creature lives and acts in isolation from, or independence of, Him; and upon the life and freedom of no creature can the divine concern fall as an unnatural and violent intrusion. To create and to be unreservedly concerned for and with the creation are indissoluble and integral aspects of the divine life; and apart from this creativity and this sustaining and re-creative concern the creature is nothing and its destiny is blank. But at the same time theism teaches the uniqueness of man as free rational spirit. Man, too, is a purposer. He too is a will. And the fulfillment of his nature means the widest possible exercise of his freedom, and this *he* must do. Therefore whatever of arbitrary restriction man makes for himself in unjust and coercive private habits and social institutions, must be rooted out. What denies freedom and corrupts and besmirches and cheapens human worth and dignity, must be resisted to the last ditch—and beyond. And if there is a deeper malignant growth upon human freedom and power, deeper than the eye can follow in the heart and will of every man, we should be sustained by nothing but the hope that he who searches the inward part will have mercy and will redeem us all from that destroyer. Beyond this in the direction of specifying how God acts in and upon the finite will, that its true destiny might be fulfilled, theism is not compelled to go. He who goes further, goes by faith in the "memory" and the hopes of the concrete historical religious community, the fellowship of believers.

Finally, theism is not compelled to absolutize the moral principles of any one cutural epoch. It does not include a specific and detailed description of the cosmic moral order strangely similar to the moral expectations of the contemporary society. The world is a place for "soul making"; and what contributes to that and what obstructs that, must be discovered by man himself, and this he does with painful tardiness. It would seem, though, that in spite of the tardiness, he has learned some things, and not merely made a guess about them that will have to be revised if the atmosphere cools off a little. In our own time, for instance, we are making the painful discovery that the "relativizing" of all moral values and moral claims spells the dissolution of those claims and the transvaluation of those values for many persons, rightly or wrongly. Morality for them—and their name is legion—is what the state demands, or what taste permits, or what will support the American way. Truth is elbowed hard by ideology; and morality by expediency; and justice by power. The good and the criteria of the good become the functions of political geography, or of scientific method, the prime operational presupposition of which is the insulation of observation and judgment from all valuational concern.

This can hardly be the way to "humanize" values, or to make the good and the true and the beautiful relevant ideals, or to enrich and empower the human enterprise: this is the cure about which there are no complaints, because the patient does not survive its application.

VI. The Ghost of Religion

I WANT TO SHOW in this concluding chapter that humanism is not a religion at all in the proper sense and that therefore the acceptance of humanism means the abandonment and abolition of the religious enterprise as such. I cannot pretend to know whether future generations will adopt this course; but I shall venture the opinion that if they do so, it will be part of a comprehensive process of the "dehumanization" of humanity.

Humanism is not a religion at all in the proper sense,[1] because for one thing its ethics (its analysis and proclamation of the good) is divorced from cosmology or is associated only vaguely with an inherently ambiguous cosmology. Accordingly humanism encourages man to take something (in this case himself) with the utmost seriousness without offering him a clear conception of where he stands in the whole picture, and thus humanism leaves us without the basic knowledge of whether we are coming or going. On the other hand, fully-developed or organic religion provides instruction on that very important question. The religions differ greatly here, that is true, but the question cannot be ignored for that or any other reason.

In the second place, humanism is but a fragment of religion because it affords inadequate scope for the play of *imagination* in

---

[1] The fact that it is preached from Christian pulpits does not contradict this. Everything from Marxist social philosophy to essays on the sanitary practices of primitive Semites is also proclaimed from that pulpit. Many times the content of the pulpit utterance reveals clearly only what seminary the preacher attended and at what time.

aesthetic, moral and speculative interests, as far as these are woven into the religious life.

Imagination in religion has both a serious and a non-serious side, and in both it enriches and embellishes the religious life. In more primitive religion the dance, whatever its serious undertone, everywhere reveals the "over-plus" of aesthetic (and occasionally the fun-loving) imagination. The dance survives in "high religion," as we see it about us, as ritual and liturgy, as formalized gesture, tone, etc. And in the highest liturgical forms we again encounter the "over-plus" of pure aesthetic imagination. Now and then theological doctrine or ecclesiastical practice slips a harsh choke-collar upon the aesthetic imagination, but sooner or later it eludes such arbitrary restraints; or if it does not, that religion or sect loses its vitality and its vividness.

The religiously concerned imagination also functions with magnificent results in the realm of poetry, producing the ageless myths and narratives of Hebrew religion, the mighty epics of Christian vision such as *The Divine Comedy* and *Paradise Lost,* and the superb cadences of The Book of Common Prayer and the King James translation of the Bible.

Why is such creativity in the imagination unlikely in such religious expression as humanism affords? Because there is nothing that can really gain from such embellishment, there is no mystery that requires or can profitably employ such expression. Humanism is primarily an ethics, or a call to social-ethical activity. It *demands* something; it *prescribes* something: it *promises* nothing. Religion (I am obviously thinking of the Christian faith especially) also knows the imperative mood, but it promises something as well—"Seek me and ye shall live." It promises life under optimum and maximum conditions, and it freely acknowledges that the character and the power and the glory of that life can be adequately represented, if at all, only by the imagination ("And I John saw the Heavenly City"). But not so humanism. Humanism is religion without liturgy and without appeal to the production of the aesthetic "over-plus"; and it is therefore but a fragment, a disjointed part, of religion.

Thirdly, humanism is not a religion in the full sense because it strikes for a minimum settlement rather than for the maximum, for "life under optimum conditions." Much of the humanist's time is spent on getting us put straight *on what we must learn to do without:* we can't count on heaven, or on divine love and justice, or on any bed-rock unshakeable values, or on any necessary truths. Our three score years and ten are the full cut, and we are lucky to get it, and the only friend in the world that man has is himself (and a fair-weather friend he is too). Man is up from a slob of protoplasm that had an incurable itch, and he is going strictly nowhere, and in a hurry. But, the humanist says, get in there and fight. In contrast to all of this, "organic" religion, full-bodied faith, declares that the beatitude of the "faithful," however defined and discerned, is incomparably richer than we can dream and is fully worth the price of these present afflictions. *If it does anything at all, it persuades men not to settle out of court for anything they can get but to sue for the greatest conceivable good.* This is of course risky business; and so is every great and greatly productive enterprise.

Humanism is not then a religion at all in the full or organic sense. We might, it is true, have made this part of our objective easier by simply insisting that where no urge to worship is acknowledged, no religion can be said to exist. And in the humanistic perspective there is nothing to worship, nothing before which to stand in awe and reverence, no sense of the holy. The supreme object of human loyalty is human value; but very few, if any, contemporary humanists, would take that to mean that humanity ought to be worshipped. Not since poor, mad Comte has humanism wandered into that dead-end street. Then there is nothing for it but to view the urge to worship as either the urge to "poetize" human life, or as the suvival of primitive mental habits that ought now to be corrected. In either case, the nerve of genuine and productive worship has been severed, for that nerve is the consciousness of the reality of the one worshipped.

The substitution of this fragment for "organic" religion would mean the abandonment and abolition of the religious enterprise. There are humanists who are quite prepared for this and who would welcome this as a most salutary advance. It would be the fully explicit acknowledgement that man has no cosmic allies and his credo must be: "Man for and by himself!"

This "advance" is advance towards the "dehumanization" of man, and this for two reasons. First, it calls for the destruction of a profoundly human interest and activity. Here humanism adds nothing; it subtracts. I do not understand this to mean that there is a "religious instinct" which atrophies if not exercised. It is true that religion is an organic feature of every high and productive culture but this does not argue "instinct." It argues at least a dim apprehension of the "wider environment" and its bearing upon human concerns. And so religion is a barrier against the complete theoretical diremption of human values and the world—the whole of nature or the universe. Religion dimly apprehends the whole of things and tries to relate the spirit most productively to this whole. Humanism calls for the repudiation of all such apprehension. It either rules out all significant knowledge of cosmic patterns or judges that human values have no significant productive relationship with such patterns. And here humanism stands revealed as inveterately parochial in its doctrine and its preachments. Whatever of poetry it may conjure to grace and to comfort or to purify and to ennoble man's passage through brute nature, must ultimately prove illusion. It may draw upon sonnet or lyric in which the inefficacious realm of emotion and desire are hymned; but not upon the stirring epic in which is sung the high and fateful encounter of spirit with its cosmic allies and foes.

A view of life and a prescription for life incurably provincial cannot dignify and enrich the human spirit, and such a view is not creatively religious whether or not it can pass muster as philosophical. Humanism says, at least through Professor Auer: Pause not to ask, Whence? or Why? or Whither? But rather be assured that Thou art alone in infinite, silent Nature. And go spend and be spent that this reeling asylum of goodness and wisdom may be enriched ere it is submerged.

A second reason for believing that humanism is a step towards the "dehumanization" of the human spirit is that it deprives the pursuit of the good life of adequate motivation and thereby casts a pall of meaninglessness over the whole show.

It is common knowledge that theistic religion, including certain historical phases of Christianity, have overworked certain motivations for the pursuit of the good, such as hope of eternal bliss or fear of unending torment. These have very likely been overworked even where the metaphysical presuppositions entirely substantiated *some* appeal to them.[2] Nevertheless, the *intent* in such appeals must be honored, and that intent is to show that the question of the destiny of the self has a great deal to do with the concrete content of the good life, with the way men go about the business of living. Humanism appears to deny this, either by trying to rule the question out of bounds or by asserting that the certainty of annihilation of the spirit should not jeopardize the enthusiasm of our appreciation and pursuit of values so long as we—and they—last. But the first attitude is purely arbitrary, and the second, as it stands, is simply an impossible requirement for most, if not all, of us. Indeed, I should say that as an *imperative* it has no sense at all.

Humanist literature, on the whole, is a fair testimony to the impossibility of this requirement. Whoever has enquired of theistic religion at its best (which I believe is the Christian faith)

---

[2] All such ethical sanctions would necessarily be improper where it was known that heaven and hell were fictions. The humanist does not always profess to know this, and therefore presumably he believes that the probabilities lie against their reality. But if *any* probability remains on the side of heaven and hell, which attitude is sounder, the humanist's, or Pascal's?

what boons, what great and precious things God promises, what "inexhaustible riches" are in store for those who persevere in faith, hope and love, can, I believe, hardly restrain himself from crying out, "That's for me!", or, "There, by the grace of God, go I!" But some believe that such great things are unattainable, for the God who alone could guarantee them does not exist, or He is silent or absent. Therefore, they say, hope for such blessedness must be abandoned; and a more modest, a lower-flying aim is set, and a diminution of enthusiasm for the "fitness of things" ensues. What is proffered at the end, as a reasonable and manageable aim, is to do one's duty to the race, in this finding fulfillment of self, and withal neither to bless nor to curse the wide, wide world about us. And thus over the ethical, as over the religious quest, there falls the gray and uncertain light cast by the conviction that even stern duty faithfully done receives from the world that spawned us no greater recompense or recognition than is meted out to the recreant, the coward and the fool. I, for one, cannot believe that this is the light that quickens and nourishes both high aspiration and the joyous acceptance of life and freedom.

A case against humanism is not proof positive for something else. In the earlier chapters that positive case has been discussed. In this chapter I have been satisfied to point out ways in which humanism cannot pass muster as a religion and therefore cannot be reasonably defended as a substitute for theistic Christianity. Finally, one does well, I believe, to interpret humanism as a protest against complacency in erroneous and inadequate expressions of positive and theistic Christian faith. Christianity *has* sometimes been so presented that man was left an alien on these shores, with no legitimate concern for this world but to get out of it with a whole soul. The correction of this and all similar errors is not, however, to make man a greater alien still, albeit in the name of helping him mature. The correction is to see men in their organic relatedness as *persons,* as rational, purposeful selves, to the cosmic pattern. It is to know ourselves caught up in processes, patterns and laws that *make for righteousness and freedom on purpose;* and to see the purpose in the mind and will and heart of God. This is theism.

CHGO SCHOOL OF THEOLOGY

S. J. CASE
S MATHEWS
GB SMITH
JMP SMITH
ES AMES
GB FOSTER

ALFRED NORTH WHITEHEAD

CHARLES HARTSHORNE

HENRY NELSON WIEMAN

BERNARD McDOUGALL LOOMER

DANIEL DAY WILLIAMS

NORMAN PITTINGER

JOHN COBB

BERNARD E. MELAND

SCHUBERT OGDEN

W. BARNETT BLAKEMORE

DUNCAN LITTLEFAIR

D.C. MACINTOSH